THE EDGE

ENDORSEMENTS

"This book is life changing—the cutting-edge to win in a high-pressure, dog-eat-dog world. Candidly sharing their personal struggles, Pastor Dave and Joanne communicate insights for turning weaknesses into strengths. Filled with clear teaching from God's Word, they connect truth for life's ups and downs."

John Thune
United States Senator

"*The Edge* has the backbone of real insight for life change that only comes from forty-plus years of ministry. Dave and Joanne have put together a study that offers hope and change for those places we all struggle. So many of us have a sense that there is a victorious life of faith that seems just out of our reach. Through the reading, individual exercises, and small group discussion this study will show you how God brings that life of promise within your grasp."

Pastor Tom Holladay
Teaching Pastor
Saddleback Church, Lake Forest, California

"This book is the best Bible study I have read that explains how to live the Christian life. The book is full of examples that demonstrate the power of living out the teachings of Jesus. It describes how to apply Biblical teaching in practical and useful ways that will impact your life and those around you."

Craig Kitchens
Movie Producer and President
Hometown Studio and Distribution

"The church today is in dire need of Bible study material that not only well informs the mind with truth but equally targets to transform the heart. *The Edge* by Dave and Joanne Beckwith scores the highest marks on both accounts. Each chapter is biblically insightful, the exercises personally practical, and the group discussions designed to cultivate authentic believer community. This book is life transforming."

Pastor Lou Damiani
Church Discipleship Ministries
The Navigators

"We all have weaknesses and shortcomings in our lives that unless addressed can undermine our efforts and sabotage our success. Based on their personal life experiences and the solid teaching of Scripture, Dave and Joanne Beckwith present a practical plan for helping us face our flaws and turn our liabilities into assets. If you are serious about making real changes in your life, this book is for you."

Dr. Gary Tangeman
Lead Pastor
Celebration Church, Santa Ana, California

"Dave was a leader ... starting in his student days at Biola University and Talbot Seminary. His love for God's Word and desire to share Christ were evident as a pastor, conference director, and mission's leader. Dave and Joanne's life theme is 'God's awesome power displayed in our weakness.' I guarantee you'll be blessed by this book."

Ron Hafer
Chaplain (Retired)
Biola University

"I have enjoyed friendship and in-depth spiritual conversation with Dave and Joanne Beckwith for over thirty years. Their insights always open my eyes to see God more clearly and love him more dearly. As you delve into their writings, I know you will be greatly blessed and deeply challenged in very practical ways to grow in your walk with God."

Kitty Jones
Women's Bible Study Author and Teacher

THE EDGE

God's Power Perfected in Weakness

A Six-week Personal Growth Journey

Dave and Joanne Beckwith

Elk Lake
PUBLISHING

Elk Lake Publishing

THE EDGE: God's Power Perfected in Weakness
Copyright © 2015 by Dave and Joanne Beckwith

Requests for information should be addressed to:
Elk Lake Publishing, Atlanta, GA 30024
ISBN-13 NUMBER: 978-1-942513-66-7

All rights reserved. No part of this publication, either text or image may be used for any purpose other than personal use. Therefore, reproduction, modification, storage in a retrieval system or retransmission, in any form or by any means, electronic, mechanical or otherwise, for reasons other than personal use, except for brief quotations in reviews or articles and promotions, is strictly prohibited without prior written permission from the publisher.

Cover and graphics design: Anna O'Brien
Editing: Jerry Gramckow, Kathi Macias, and Deb Haggerty
Published in association with Steve Hutson/WordWise Media

Unless otherwise noted, all Scripture is taken from:
Holy Bible, New International Version®, NIV® Copyright ©1973, 1978, 1984, 2011 by Biblica, Inc.® Used by permission. All rights reserved worldwide.

Also used:
** The Message (MSG) Copyright © 1993, 1994, 1995, 1996, 2000, 2001, 2002 by Eugene H. Peterson
** J. B. Phillips, "The New Testament in Modern English," (Phillips NT) Copyright 1962 edition by HarperCollins
** Holy Bible. New Living Translation (NLT) Copyright© 1996, 2004, 2007, 2013 by Tyndale House Foundation. Used by permission of Tyndale House Publishers Inc., Carol Stream, Illinois 60188. All rights reserved.
** New American Standard Bible (NASB) Copyright © 1960, 1962, 1963, 1968, 1971, 1972, 1973, 1975, 1977, 1995 by The Lockman Foundation
** Contemporary English Version (CEV) Copyright © 1991, 1992, 1995 by American Bible Society
** New Century Version (NCV) The Holy Bible, New Century Version®. Copyright © 2005 by Thomas Nelson, Inc.
** The Living Bible (TLB) Copyright © 1971 by Tyndale House Foundation. Used by permission of Tyndale House Publishers Inc., Carol Stream, Illinois 60188. All rights reserved.

TABLE OF CONTENTS

	Page
Dedication	9
Preface: Jim and Debbie Hogan	11
Introduction: A Forty-day Personal Growth Journey	13
The Edge	17
Chapter One: When Life Hits You Head-on	19
Chapter Two: Why Did God Design Me with Weaknesses?	49
Chapter Three: Changing My Mind	89
Chapter Four: Releasing Resentments	137
Chapter Five: Releasing Regrets	171
Chapter Six: Why Can't You Be More Like Me?	205
Your Edge to Thrive	245
Appendix A: Three Simple Steps to New Life	247
Appendix B: A Guide for Small Groups	249
Appendix C: Digging Deeper in Psalm 119	259
Appendix D: Releasing Resentments	261
Appendix E: Releasing Regrets	263
Changing My Mind Verses	265
About the Authors	267
Endnotes	269
Scripture Index	275

To our daughters

Julie Ann McGough

and

Tamara Dawn Baker

Travelers with us in many of our life adventures

They are both lovely, godly women who bring us much joy.

We thank God for them, and their love, encouragement, and support.

PREFACE

This book is about change and the *edge* it can give you when God changes you. Change isn't always easy or fun, but it is necessary to help us become the men and women God wants us to be. The purpose of *THE EDGE: God's Power Perfected in Weakness* is to unlock the principles for life transformation through discovering God's strength in human weakness.

In a world where we are being told "only the strong survive," Dave and Joanne Beckwith give us a refreshing paradigm shift by going against the flow and reminding us of God's promise: *He gives strength to the weary and increases the power of the weak* (Isa. 40:29). Using the life lessons they've learned through their many years of ministry, marriage, and living, Dave and Joanne give a practical guide to gain an edge in your life by allowing the Lord to refine you by using your weaknesses. It is in times of our darkest hours, our worst failures, and our greatest struggles that the Lord is refining us. This book will give you insights that can help you:

- Release resentments and regrets
- Control negative thought patterns
- Learn how to grow from your weaknesses
- Stop being intimidated and become God-empowered
- Learn the ABC's to free others to change

If you want to gain an *edge* on life by allowing the Lord to make some positive changes, do yourself a favor and begin reading and applying what you are about to learn from this book. You'll be glad you did!

Jim and Debbie Hogan
Co-founders of Standing Stone Ministry
Authors of *Shepherding Shepherds: The Standing Stone Story*

INTRODUCTION

A FORTY-DAY PERSONAL GROWTH JOURNEY

Are there areas in your life that need transformation? Would you like to experience more of the power of God? This forty-day personal growth journey is written to provide insights and deepen your walk with God and experience his power in new ways.

God has done some amazing things in forty days. He gave Moses the Ten Commandments during forty days on Mt. Sinai (Ex. 24:18). Elijah traveled forty days to Mt. Sinai where he had a life-changing encounter with God (1 Kings 19:8). Jonah preached for forty days and the great city of Nineveh repented (Jon. 3:4). Jesus fasted for forty days and nights before the start of his public ministry (Matt. 4:2). After his death and resurrection, Jesus showed himself alive for forty days, appearing to more than five hundred before his ascension into heaven (Acts 1:3).

What will God do in your life in the next forty days? This book is designed as a forty-day, six-week personal growth journey—a unique opportunity to discover God's power for your weaknesses. You will discover most weaknesses have a hidden, camouflaged strength: the perfectionist has the potential to be productive as well as thorough; those who grieve can develop a unique capacity to give comfort; and the reckless renegade can become a courageous champion for what is right.

Different than STRENGTHS FINDER, the popular Gallup assessment to discover your natural abilities and aptitudes, this is STRENGTHS BUILDER—God's power in human weakness that confounds the wisdom of the world and the power of the elite.

> *Human strength can't begin to compete with God's "weakness." Take a good look, friends, at who you were when you got called into this life. I don't see many of "the brightest and the best" among you, not many influential, not many from high-society families. Isn't it obvious that God deliberately chose men and women that the culture overlooks and exploits and abuses, chose these "nobodies" to expose the hollow pretensions of the "somebodies"?* (1 Cor. 1:25-28 MSG)

This is hope for the disillusioned and disappointed, the so-called "nobodies." Take heart. God displays his power in weakness. The deeply wounded are shaped into healers, the discarded become lifters of the downtrodden, the greedy become givers, and rebels become godly leaders.

Marriages, as well as friendships, grow deeper with an understanding of strengths and weaknesses. In relationships, opposites attract, but they also "rub," creating an agenda to change the other person. Is it possible to change someone you love? No. Changing a life is God's business, but you can be used by God to help someone change by cooperating with God's work in their life and becoming a STRENGTHS BUILDER.

This book is designed for reading one chapter each week; however, proceed at your own pace. A meditation verse is included for each week. Carry it with you, direct your thoughts to it frequently throughout the day, and memorize it for maximum benefit. The chapters also include five daily "Time Outs" for your personal quiet time. Each day, read a short section until you come to the "Time Out." Stop there, read the Scripture included, seek the Lord in prayer, and apply what you've read.

Ask a few friends to join you as you read, and you'll have a "Strength Team" for interaction, support, and encouragement. Each chapter includes materials for a small group. This is the "Strength Team" guide, and each lesson includes five sections designed for healthy group life: Connect, Grow, Apply, Pray, and Share.

For clarification as you read, the chapters are primarily written by Dave unless noted otherwise. Joanne took the lead in writing the "Time Outs" and the "Strength Team" materials for small groups.

Our heartfelt thanks to those who have encouraged us on the journey and provided wise counsel. Authors and freelance editors Kathi Macias and Kathi Ide taught the first all-day writing workshop I attended seven years ago. I thought I was a decent writer until they helped me see how much I had to learn. It has been a privilege to have Kathi Macias as one of the editors of this book. She is a multi-award winning writer who has authored more than fifty books and ghostwritten several others. Friend to friend, she has given gentle correction and frequent encouragement. Steve Hutson, Literary Agent with WordWise Media, worked diligently to find the right publisher while providing frequent encouragement and guidance. Editor Jerry Gramckow provided his incredible scrutiny regarding the structure and grammar. It's tough to get anything past his keen eye for details, but I including this sentence just to show it be done anyhow. Deb Haggerty, a professional editor and Senior Vice President of Acquisitions for Elk Lake, put the finishing touches on the book. I am also grateful to the team leading Orange County Christian Writers who have provided a yearly conference with speakers and workshops where I have learned so much. Rich and Karen Thune, Maria Martinez, Lou Damiani, and others have helped out by reading and editing selected sections. Our thanks to Woodbridge Community Church for providing a test group for the small group materials. And a big thank you to our tech-savvy grandson, Sean McGough, who has repeatedly rescued us when we were ready to throw our computers off a cliff.

Just before this book went to print, Don Klassen, whose story is at the end of Chapter Two, passed from this life into the presence of the Lord. We're glad we could include his story as a testimony to his life. Our compassion and love to Sharon, his wonderful wife.

Enjoy discovering your "edge." We pray God will give you the "cutting-edge" to overcome and win in this high-pressure, dog-eat-dog world.

Pastor Dave and Joanne Beckwith

THE EDGE ...

... the cutting side of a blade,

... the threshold of danger or ruin,

... vigor and energy,

... keenness and intensity of desire,

... a favorable margin,

... an advantage.[1]

Welcome to "the edge." I live here. Teetering on the precipice, always a step from danger, I do my balancing act. Often tired and weak, I tap in to divine energy—dancing with delight and enjoying a "cutting-edge" to win.

My struggle has always been that wherever I go, *there I am*. I polished the art of blaming others, but when my excuses ran out, I had to look in the mirror and admit—I was the problem. As someone observed, "If I could kick my worst enemy in the seat of the pants, I wouldn't be able to sit down for a week." That's me.

I was always hoping others would applaud my strengths. Some did but not for long. My weaknesses—faults, flaws, and inadequacies— were like the "sharp edge of a blade," cutting into my fragile sense of worth, leaving me disappointed, wounded, and bleeding. No, I was never a drug user, compulsive gambler, hatemonger, inside-trader, or murderer. Instead, manipulating and conniving to get my way, gluttony, resentment, hypocrisy, self-centeredness, out-of-control compulsiveness, and perfectionism derailed me over and over again. I lived with nagging self-disappointment.

Unchecked, my weaknesses could have led me to "the edge of ruin." I have often wondered what my life would be like if I hadn't been arrested by Christ. I surmise I'd be working in the business world, married three or four times, addicted to who knows what, having children who wouldn't even talk to me, and burned out on life—that is, if I were still alive. A greater likelihood is that I would have died in my fifties like my father and grandfather.

Through the process of experiencing brokenness and discovering the power of Christ in my weaknesses, my life today is filled with the "cutting-edge" of vigor and energy and "the sharpened-edge" of intense desire. My weaknesses have become "power points" to the glory of God.

Weaknesses empowered by God are a winner's edge, a distinct advantage. Paul, a radically reshaped man, leveraged "the edge." Coming to terms with an agonizing weakness, Paul heard the Lord say, *My power is strongest when you are weak* (2 Cor. 12:9 CEV). Paul discovered the power-edge—the favorable margin to overcome seemingly insurmountable obstacles. His mantra: *When I am weak, I am strong* (v. 10).

Living "the edge" is changing my life, and it will do the same for you. Come join me in the pursuit of the "winning-edge"—God's strength in weakness.

Dave Beckwith

CHAPTER ONE

WHEN LIFE HITS YOU HEAD-ON

I was trying to do it myself—while God was trying to bring me to the end of myself.

With the shrill sound of sirens, the smell of burning fuel, and flames piercing through the black darkness, I regained consciousness. Where was I? What was going on? Slowly I realized I was lying in the middle of the freeway. Then I remembered the two headlights coming straight at me! As I drifted in and out of consciousness, I heard my wife's voice, calm in assurance and deep in faith, reciting Psalm 23. *Even though I walk through the valley of the shadow of death, I fear no evil, for you are with me.* God had spared my life.

The dramatic series of events leading up to and following this fateful day started me on a journey that would forever change my life. I began to realize that life—and all its drama—was sometimes beyond my control. It was one of the first times I felt completely weak and helpless to deal with what was happening around me. But it wouldn't be the last.

The Rest of the Story

During the early morning hours of August 30, 1970, California Highway Patrol officers Gary Haley and Tom Long were performing routine duties patrolling the freeway between Ventura and Santa Paula,

California. They followed several cars and prepared to stop one for speeding. Suddenly the officers noticed cars ahead of them slowing and veering erratically, some swerving right, others left. Then they saw two headlights coming straight at them. It was a nightmare before their eyes—a wrong-way driver on the freeway.

A few minutes earlier, with a blood alcohol level of 0.18, the driver of a compact sedan had entered the freeway off-ramp driving head-on into the oncoming traffic. As she approached the police car, Officer Long turned on the electronic siren while Officer Haley aimed the spotlight at her to get her attention and yelled for her to pull over using the PA system. Anyone in their right mind could see the glaring spotlight and flashing red lights. Was she trying to commit suicide? She responded like a mummy in a tomb. Looking straight ahead, she kept driving into oncoming traffic. How long could this go on? Death—hers and perhaps innocent others—was inevitable if she weren't stopped immediately.

Traffic was too heavy for Officer Long to turn the patrol vehicle around. In desperation, he tried backing up along the shoulder of the freeway while steering clear of oncoming traffic. It was no use. They were quickly losing her. Then, finding an opening in the center divider, he shot across to the other side of the freeway and raced in an attempt to catch her. Once parallel, they continued flashing warnings at her for several miles. "We could see her ... almost like sitting next to her," Haley said. "The red and white lights still did no good. I got on the outside PA system and started screaming at her to get over. He [Long] got on the electronic siren. She just continued looking straight ahead, driving up the freeway in the wrong direction. She never once turned to look." When the futility of their chase became obvious, Haley and Long attempted to warn oncoming traffic. Despite their efforts, two approaching vehicles could not see the warning lights ahead.

At 1:40 a.m., I was driving one of those oncoming cars, returning from a youth trip to a Dodgers' baseball game. My passengers included my wife, Joanne, and four teenagers—Jerry Reich, Dennis Sprik, Larry Thiesen, and John Sigala. For several miles, an off-duty sheriff's deputy named Dan Bowlin drove sidebyside in the lane next to me. Through the window, I could see the badge on his uniform as I kept a close eye on my speedometer. Ahead was a gentle, rolling hill—a familiar, welcoming site indicating home was just a few miles farther.

THE EDGE

Suddenly, without warning, over the top of the hill, I saw two headlights coming straight at me. The glare was blinding. Officer Bowlin, traveling in the right lane, swerved to safety. Panicked, I swerved right but too late. The small compact car crashed into the left front of the car I was driving. The screaming, screeching sound of metal clashing and bending pierced the night as the two vehicles collided at a combined speed of a 130 miles per hour. The compact sedan was crushed like a cardboard box, killing the driver instantly.

"My God! They hit headon!" Haley yelled. Officer Long raced through the center divider with the patrol vehicle. Haley and Long jumped out of the car and ran toward us. Joanne crawled out of the car with blood streaming down her face and staggered toward the officers screaming, "Help us! Oh, my God, help us!" Two of the teenagers had managed to escape the car. The other two were in the back, one on the car seat, the other on the floor. Unconscious, I was trapped behind the mangled steering wheel.

Officer Haley crawled into the backseat of the car, pulling one teenager to safety as flames leaped from the engine compartment. Officer Long grabbed the fire extinguisher, shooting it at the flames to no avail. Haley then carried the other teenager to safety as the flames continued to spread. Five had been rescued; one was left in the car.

With the engine compartment in flames, the car obviously could explode at any moment. I was not only trapped behind the steering wheel, but the driver's side door was crushed. The officer yelled, "We've got to get him out of there." Realizing I was still in the car, Joanne crawled in the passenger side desperately working to pull me free from the burning vehicle. The strength of the crushed door certainly exceeded human strength. Special equipment would be required to open it. There was no time for a jaws-of-life rescue.

A pool of gasoline had spilled under and around the car. Aware they were walking in gasoline and risking their lives as the flames continued to spread, Dennis Sprik, one of the rescued teenagers, and Officers Haley and Bowlin approached the car. They put their full strength into opening the driver's side door that wouldn't budge. Dennis said the leaping flames from the engine compartment stopped short of the windshield, almost as if there were an invisible wall holding the flames back. Then a trail of gasoline from the car caught fire. The car would explode in seconds. In one final attempt, they pulled on the door, and it opened. As the smoke and heat grew in intensity, they grabbed me: "I couldn't extract Beckwith," Haley recalled. "If we didn't get him out, he was going to go. He was screaming. I knew I was hurting him, but I'd rather have him hurt than dead. The car was burning, and I was trying to get him out as best I could." With a final jerk, they pulled me free from the mangled dash and crumpled steering wheel pinning me inside the car. Just seconds later, as they laid me on the pavement, the car exploded in an inferno of flames. My eternal gratitude overflows to those who risked their lives to rescue me from the burning car. Officers Tom Long, Gary Haley, and Dan Bowlin each received the "Certificate of Accommodation for Meritorious Achievement" in recognition of their courage and bravery risking their lives in the line of duty. My life-long friend, Dennis Sprik, also risked his life in the rescue.[2]

As Joanne held me close during the ambulance ride to the hospital, I drifted in and out of consciousness. From adjoining beds in the emergency room, we discovered the physical injuries each had suffered. I was writhing in pain with lacerations to my legs and chest, several broken teeth, and a broken wrist. I also had deep puncture wounds to both sides of my neck. Amazingly, the neck wounds hadn't lacerated the jugular veins. Joanne suffered a deep cut through her left cheek that went to the bone only a fraction of an inch from her eye. The surgery required three layers of stitches, but her eyesight was spared.

Once released from the hospital, we came face to face with our challenges: we were unemployed, with about $200 in savings, private school tuition to pay, medical bills in the thousands, no car, and a baby to feed and care for. We were grateful our two-month-old daughter, Julie, was with a babysitter the night of the accident.

Over the next few months, things went from bad to worse. Life was spinning wildly, and we were struggling to hang on. Physically, we were banged up and continued to be in pain. Emotionally, we were drained and discouraged. Financially, we were sinking, and our parents were in no position to assist us with medical expenses and college costs. Spiritually, we were at the end of our "hope rope." Little did we know this was exactly where God wanted us. He had lessons to teach us in our weakness.

Day One Time Out

Power Thoughts for Your Time Alone with God

We were at the end of our "hope rope." Little did we know this was exactly where God wanted us. He had lessons to teach us in our weakness.

- Read Psalm 23, the chapter Joanne quoted after Dave's rescue from the burning car. Could you quote it to someone going through *the valley of the shadow of death* (v. 4)? As it has only six verses, this is a great chapter to commit to memory.

- Think of a time when you were at the end of your "hope rope." What was God teaching you?

- How does this Psalm speak to you regarding your past, present, and future?

- As you go back through Psalm 23, personalize it and pray the thoughts back to God. "My Lord, you are my shepherd. How awesome that you watch over me. You are aware of my every want, and you supply my every need."

Dave and Joanne Beckwith

From the Frying Pan into the Fire

The catastrophic car accident was just the beginning. In the months that followed, I found myself questioning God again and again: "Why is this happening?" An inexplicable series of setbacks invaded our lives. Our insurance company notified us our auto insurance rates would go up because I now had an accident on my record. "What? This isn't fair!" I protested to the insurance agent to no avail.

Since we were without a vehicle, Joanne's parents lent us a car. Less than a week later and in a rush to get to an appointment, I couldn't find the car. After searching the parking area and talking to the apartment manager to make sure no one had towed it, I realized it had been stolen. Sinking in despair, I stood looking at the empty spot where I'd parked the car, asking God, "With car number-one burned and totaled and car number-two stolen, what are we supposed to do? Walk?" We filed a police report, but the car was never recovered. Joanne's dad didn't have it insured for theft, so we owed Joanne's parents for the stolen car, and we were still without an automobile.

As medical bills arrived stamped "Due and Payable Now," all I could do was stare in utter disbelief. The depression was overwhelming as the bills, mounting to thousands of dollars, buried us in debt. Meanwhile, I needed major dental reconstruction due to the broken teeth. Confused and disheartened, my attitude turned sour.

A week after the car was stolen, the stereo in our apartment caught fire, blackening the stair railing and walls. The fire and smoke also reignited the memories and fears of the accident.

A few weeks later, my billfold was stolen. Someone enjoyed a spending spree using our credit cards. Angry and resentful, I became obsessed with trying to track down and confront this person.

Joanne's dad lent us the money to buy a used car to get by but we still had no money and no job. A few months prior to the accident, I had graduated from Biola with my Bachelor of Science degree in Business Administration. During my college years, I had received affirmation as a student leader and assumed the business world was excitedly awaiting my arrival. I was in for a big disappointment. I began applying for positions with various businesses, thinking some company would certainly want me as a junior executive. The Chairman of the Biola Business Department, Bob Livingston, assured me a position would open up soon. For two months, I pursued every lead. To my dismay, I couldn't even get an interview. Finally, Bob Livingston called to say he had a job opening.

"What company?" I asked.

"Dart Transportation in Los Angeles."

"All right, finally, an interview," I replied. "What's the position and salary?"

"This may not be your dream position," Bob said, "but they have an opening for loading trucks on the evening shift. It pays a little over minimum wage. You'll be working on the dock, loading Sears' freight for Dart Transportation."

What? A college degree so I could load trucks at night? My disappointment was obvious on the phone, but I needed a job. I went for the interview and got hired. During the year that followed, I worked the loading dock from 3:30 p.m. until all the freight was loaded—usually midnight, but sometimes 2 or 3 a.m. Biola classes for Joanne and Talbot Seminary classes for me started at 7:30 a.m. and dismissed at noon. Our infant daughter, Julie, stayed with a wonderful friend during the morning. When classes dismissed, we picked Julie up and shared a brief lunch together before studying and heading back to work.

I'd always been able to pull things through by relying on my strengths. But at this point, my strengths were no match for the avalanche of life problems. I began to face the fact that I was not only weak but had a lot of weaknesses. I became fearful, discouraged, and resentful. Joanne, struggling with vivid memories of the head-on crash and exploding car, experienced fear, which she shares in this next section.

Spinning Out of Control

[Joanne speaking] The Cinderella story I'd envisioned for my life became a nightmare. Over and over, my mind replayed the sounds of crushing metal and blaring sirens. It brought to mind the many attempts to pull Dave from the car, followed by the explosion, and finally wondering if Dave would die as he lay there on the pavement. My sleep was interrupted by fearful thoughts and dreams.

I had difficulty feeling safe in a car and even felt vulnerable in our home, repeatedly checking the closets for intruders. Whenever I caught the smell of smoke, it set off an adrenaline surge, and my mind froze. When our home stereo caught fire and smoke poured out the back, I was paralyzed with panic. Something had happened to me; life seemed wildly out of control.

The refining process of purifying my faith was set in motion in my life. I had to grow stronger, to learn more fully who God was and is and why I can trust him. Without this confidence, I had no real security.

Day Two Time Out

Power Thoughts for Your Time Alone with God

When troubles come your way, consider it an opportunity for great joy. (James 1:2 NLT)

- ❑ What circumstances in your life are stretching your faith? Are they perplexing? Discouraging? Do you feel beaten?

- ❑ Read James 1:2-12.

- ❑ Have you ever thought of trials and temptations as friends? Check out this paraphrase of James 1:2-5:

When all kinds of trials and temptations crowd into your lives my brothers, don't resent them as intruders, but welcome them as friends! Realize that they come to test your faith and to produce in you the quality of endurance. But let the process go on until that endurance is fully developed, and you will find you have become men of mature character with the right sort of independence. And if, in the process, any of you does not know how to meet any particular problem he has only to ask God—who gives generously to all men without making them feel foolish or guilty—and he may be quite sure that the necessary wisdom will be given him. (Phillips NT)

- ❑ As you pray ...

1. Ask God to give you a different attitude about your trials—to even welcome them.

2. Ask God to use your trials to shape and mature you.

3. Ask God for wisdom and patience to respond to each challenge.

- ❑ Go to the back of the book, and cut out or copy this week's meditation verses called "God's Power Pack." Carry this with you and meditate on these verses throughout the week as you memorize them.

Dave and Joanne Beckwith
Refining Gold

Faith grows in the struggles and pressures of life. James McConkey said it this way:

> Faith is dependence upon God. And this God-dependence only begins when self-dependence ends. And self-dependence only comes to its end, with some of us, when sorrow, suffering, affliction, broken plans and hopes bring us to that place of self-helplessness and defeat.[3]

Life is painful and perplexing—disappointments, sorrows, broken dreams and aspirations, conflicts, misunderstandings. When life is heartbreaking and agonizing, you may wonder, *Why didn't God make life a little smoother? I hope there's a reason for this pain because it doesn't make much sense.* I assure you, there *is* a purpose, a bigger plan behind the struggle.

When your dreams come tumbling down, when someone stabs you in the back, when your health deteriorates, when you try and fail, when you're abandoned and lonely, Christ invites you to himself. He has experienced pain far beyond any suffering you can comprehend, and his love for you is greater than the love of any of your friends or family. When you are wounded and hurting, read Isaiah 53—the predictions of the suffering and death of Christ—feeling the wounds he felt and applying his healing to your life: *He was pierced for our rebellion, crushed for our sins. He was beaten so we could be whole. He was whipped so we could be healed* (Isa. 53:5 NLT).

Without brokenness, it's easy to drift along—self-sufficient, seemingly strong, judgmental and self-righteous, demanding of others and often blaming them, expecting to be served rather than serving, unmoved by the pain of others, and an all-around nuisance to live with. With crushing and breaking, you become keenly aware of your weaknesses, valuing others over yourself, and yielding rights. You respond to others with graciousness, humbled by how much you have to learn. You become willing to forgive others with the awareness of your need for forgiveness, developing compassion for others when they hurt. Your faith deepens and matures. This is the process the first-century believers were going through when Peter encouraged them with these words:

THE EDGE

In this you greatly rejoice, though now for a little while you may have had to suffer grief in all kinds of trials. These have come so that your faith—of greater worth than gold, which perishes even though refined by fire—may be proved genuine and may result in praise, glory and honor when Jesus Christ is revealed. (1 Pet. 1:6-7)

The process of refining gold is a vivid illustration of God's refining process. A hunk of gold ore doesn't look like much before being refined. First in that refining process, machines called crushers reduce large chunks of ore to the size of road gravel. Crushing is the first prerequisite. In the life of a believer, God works to crush hardness and defiance. Next, the gold ore is subjected to the smelting process. Gold melts at 1948° F (1064° C). This extreme heat is necessary to remove the impurities. Smelting involves melting the gold in a furnace with a chemical mixture called flux, which combines with the impurities and floats on top of the gold. The dross can then be skimmed or poured off. Repeated heating brings the impurities to the surface, and the skimming continues until all the impurities are removed. *In the final test of pure gold, the goldsmith can see his reflection in the gold.*

When the heat is on in your life, impurities will surface—arrogance, a sour attitude, irritability, an independent streak, jealousy, substance addiction, or anger. The natural tendency is to be horrified with what comes to the surface. Disappointment in self comes from believing in self. Your failure didn't catch God off-guard. Don't beat yourself up with your failure. Be patient with yourself—God is at work. "One of God's most effective means in the process is failure. So many believers are simply frantic over the fact of failure in their lives, and they will go to all lengths in trying to hide it, ignore it, or rationalize about it."[4] Acknowledge your failure and ask God to skim it from your life. "Failure where self is concerned in our Christian life and service is allowed and often engineered by God in order to turn us completely from ourselves to his source for our life—Christ Jesus, who never fails."[5]

Heat, pressure, failure, doubts, skimming off the impurities, more heat, trials, temptations, more removing of impurities—the goldsmith knows what he's doing. *The final test is when the goldsmith, Jesus Christ, sees his perfect reflection in you. Pure gold!*

Day Three Time Out

Power Thoughts for Your Time Alone with God

Disappointment in self comes from believing in self.

- ❏ Read and reflect on 1 Peter 1:3-9.

- ❏ When have you been disappointed in yourself?

- ❏ What tends to come to the surface (lashing out, bad attitude, overeating, driving like a maniac, etc.) when the heat is on in your life?

- ❏ Ask God to skim the impurities from your life.

Exchanging Weakness for Strength

What happens when God's power is fused with our weakness is astounding. We'll say much about this in subsequent chapters, but for now, these three weakness-to-strength principles build sequentially—the first laying the foundation for the second, and the second a prerequisite for the third. This is your edge—your unique advantage to experience a God-empowered life.

Be God-secure → Be God-surrendered → Be God-strengthened

1. Be God-secure

A core belief in God—that he is in control, that he loves you and wants the best for you—provides the foundation for being God-secure. In him, you are loved, and you begin to live like someone who is loved. You carry yourself differently. You're not as rattled when others are falling apart. The approval of others becomes less important. You're moving forward and doing great ... and then it happens. You slip and fall and feel deeply disappointed. As you ask for forgiveness and sense him picking you up, you realize he wasn't shocked or surprised by your stumble. In fact, he knew it was coming. It was part of his plan to teach and shape you, even through failure. You further realize Jesus loves you on your beautiful days as well as your bummer days. You're not on probation. His love never fluctuates; it's eternal. As this love becomes deeply internalized in your psyche and incorporated into the way you live, your faith grows stronger, more secure.

Like the slow lifting of a thick fog, some of the struggles and disappointments from the past start to make sense. You begin to have a clearer picture of what happened and why, and more importantly, how God was using it to shape you. You learn to rest secure in his love.

Sometimes you'll see a surprising benefit from what seemed to be a tragedy. After the accident, Joanne's sense of smell became amazingly sharp, and her adrenalin surged when she smelled smoke. One Sunday morning, she woke up smelling smoke, which I didn't notice. She called the fire department, and they discovered a smoldering outlet in the wall. The fire department said that without her keen sense of smell, our home would have burned to the ground while we were at church.

THE EDGE

What helped Joanne grow in being God-secure? Meditating and claiming the truths in the following verses set her free from her fearful thoughts and restless sleep.

- *"Do not tremble; do not be afraid. Did I not proclaim my purposes for you long ago? You are my witnesses—is there any other God? No! There is no other Rock—not one!"* (Isa. 44:8 NLT)

- *The LORD is my rock, my fortress, and my savior; my God is my rock, in whom I find protection. He is my shield, the power that saves me, and my place of safety.* (Ps. 18:2 NLT)

- *I am the LORD, the God of all the peoples of the world. Is anything too hard for me?* (Jer. 32:27 NLT)

- *"For I know the plans I have for you,"* declares the LORD, *"plans to prosper you and not to harm you, plans to give you hope and a future."* (Jer. 29:11)

Meditate on these verses for a week and see how they change your outlook. You'll increase your faith in who God is, in his power, and in the knowledge that you can trust him. Knowledge of your awesome God and how secure you are in him will flood your thoughts.

If all of this is new to you, you may ask, "How do I begin this relationship?" It's as simple as the ABC's. There are three simple steps to being "eternally loved and secure." Go to the back of this book and look for the page titled "Three Simple Steps to New Life" (Appendix A). Secure in your new relationship, your faith can grow. The more you learn about God's character, the more God-secure you become when life hits you head-on.

Day Four Time Out

Power Thoughts for Your Time Alone with God

A core belief in God—that he is in control, that he loves you and wants the best for you—provides a foundation for being God-secure.

- ❏ Read Psalm 18:1-6.

- ❏ Make some notes of when you were highly stressed or possibly felt your life was threatened.

- ❏ On a scale of 1-5 (5 being high), how secure do you feel in the following areas:

___ My family	___ My job	___ My investments
___ My friends	___ My health	___ My traveling (auto, airplane, etc.)
___ My retirement	___ My reputation	___ My income and expenses
___ The economy	___ World events	___ My eternal destiny

- ❏ Which issues from the above list are most difficult for you?

- ❏ Look back and reflect on the verses mentioned earlier in this section (Isa. 44:8, Ps. 18:2, Jer. 32:27 and 29:11) and apply them to your greatest areas of fear. Focus on these verses as you pray.

2. Be God-surrendered

Surrender is not our usual mode of operation. Instead, when we feel insecure, we lash out, grow stubborn, sulk, or get angry—anything but surrender. This is why being God-secure precedes being God-surrendered. The stronger your core belief that God is completely reliable, the easier it will be for you to surrender your life and future to him.

In my insecurities, I was a fighter, always struggling and striving. The idea of being weak was unthinkable. When I read *power is made perfect in weakness* and *when I am weak, then I am strong* (2 Cor. 12:9, 10), I honestly didn't have a clue what these verses meant. How could weakness be the key to strength? Everything I knew argued otherwise. I believed that to succeed, I had to be strong. To conquer, I had to take control. To win, I couldn't appear weak. The success-driven model I aspired to applauded strength, charisma, self-sufficiency, and hard work. Weakness was for wimps and losers.

For many years, even with the awareness of my weaknesses, I tried to succeed in my own strength. I was always striving, trying harder, resolving to do better—still thinking I was the source of strength. When I failed, I'd berate myself rather than accept the life-changing truth: *I was trying to do it myself—while God was trying to bring me to the end of myself.*

We like to feel we can handle what comes our way. Instead, God allows huge challenges that leave us weak-kneed and wobbly—challenges like getting out of debt, completing a degree while caring for four children and holding a full-time job, dealing with chronic pain, overcoming an addiction, raising an autistic child, grieving the loss of a loved one. Does the challenge you face leave you feeling weak in the lining of your soul? Good. To the weary, God gives strength, and he increases the power of the weak (Isa. 40:29).

Being God-secure doesn't happen all at once, and learning to be God-surrendered is a process. Through the years, you'll likely repeat the steps many times—a new experience of trusting and yielding followed by renewed strength. Philippians 3:10 becomes a lived-out process: knowing Christ more deeply in the fellowship of his suffering (becoming God-secure), experiencing conformity to his death (being God-surrendered), and then knowing the power of his resurrection (being God-strengthened). Surrender is the prelude to strength; it is God's power when you're exhausted; it is God taking over when you feel you've miserably failed. Your moment of weakness is the beginning of his strength.

3. Be God-strengthened

Your personal resources are limited. Even the young grow tired and weary. Those in their prime will stumble and fall. *Those who wait upon GOD get fresh strength. They spread their wings and soar like eagles, they run and don't get tired, they walk and don't lag behind* (Isa. 40:31 MSG). God has promised his power will be perfected in your weakness.

How would you complete this sentence? *I can do everything through* _____. Some would say, "My education ... my exceptional talents ... my problem-solving abilities ... my perseverance ... my ability to work with people." Paul said, *I can do everything through Christ, who gives me strength* (Phil. 4:13 NLT). Don't overlook the three words "everything through Christ." He will supply strength for whatever is in his plan for your life.

So why not take the first step of surrender and strike the match? Surrender lights the fire of God's power.

And here's your "power pack" of promises, fuel that keeps the fire going.

> *I can do all things through him who strengthens me.*
>
> *Greater is he who is in me than he who is in the world.*
>
> *I am more than a conqueror through him who loves me.*
>
> *Absolutely nothing is impossible with God!*[6]

Claim them, repeat them, memorize them, prove them, and when life hits you head-on, thrust your arms in the air and whisper a shout:

Dave and Joanne Beckwith

God, you promised—I am more than a conqueror ... I can do all things through you ... Nothing is impossible in your strength ... You are greater than anything life throws at me!

This is your "cutting-edge" to turn weakness into victory.

Day Five Time Out

Power Thoughts for Your Time Alone with God

Strike the match. Surrender lights the fire of God's power.

❑ Read Romans 8:28-39.

❑ What phrases in this passage fill you with an overwhelming sense of being secure?

❑ Enter into worship and praise as you read and pray through verses 31-39 below.

If God is for me, who can be against me? He who did not spare his own Son, but gave him up for me—how will he not also, along with him, graciously give me all things?
Who will bring any charge against me whom God has chosen? It is God who justifies. Who is he that condemns? Christ Jesus, who died—more than that, who was raised to life—is at the right hand of God and is also interceding for me.
Who shall separate me from the love of Christ? Shall trouble or hardship or persecution or famine or nakedness or danger or sword? As it is written: "For your sake we face death all day long; we are considered as sheep to be slaughtered." No, in all these things I am more than a conqueror through him who loved me.
For I am convinced that neither death nor life, neither angels nor demons, neither the present nor the future, nor any powers, neither height nor depth, nor anything else in all creation, will be able to separate me from the love of God that is in Christ Jesus my Lord. (Rom. 8:31-39, paraphrased in the first person)

❑ Pray a prayer of surrender. Tell God you voluntarily relinquish your will to his power and authority. Make note of specific areas you are choosing to release.

STRENGTH TEAM

SESSION ONE
WHEN LIFE HITS YOU HEAD-ON

If you've tried really hard to succeed but found yourself floundering and failing, you're going to love what you discover in this session. We're going to look at how to face the tough stuff in life and what happens when God fuses his power with our weakness. Three weakness-to-strength principles will be applied: 1) be God-secure, 2) be God-surrendered, and 3) be God-strengthened. This is your edge—your unique advantage to experiencing a God-empowered life. Let's get started in this exciting session.

A Guide for Small Groups

In preparation for your first session, read the Guide for Small Groups in Appendix B. Included in that guide are tools you will find very helpful for a successful group experience:

1) **Tips for Leading a Small Group**;

2) **Tips for Hosting a Small Group**;

3) **Five Purposes for Your Group** (which explains the five sections in each group session);

4) **Small Group Guidelines** (discuss this as a group in your first session);

5) **Ask and You Shall Receive** (write down prayer requests and answers to prayer); and

6) **God's VIPs** (your group roster, with contact information).

THE EDGE

CONNECT

- [ ] Start with an "autograph-signing party." VIP's sign autographs and every person in the group is one of God's "very important persons." Hand your book around the circle and have each person sign it and include contact information (email address and phone number). Ask them to print their information since the autographs of most VIP's are impossible to read. Use the worksheet titled "God's VIPs," included in the small-group guide (Appendix B).

- [ ] As an alternative, you can have everyone put their name and contact information on a sheet of paper. After the session, have someone word process this and email it to everyone.

- [ ] As a group, read and discuss aloud the "Small-Group Guidelines" included in the small-group guide (Appendix B).

GROW

- [ ] The 23rd Psalm is one of the most loved sections in the Bible. Read Psalm 23 in the two translations below. Read around the circle, having each person read a verse.

The LORD is my shepherd, I shall not be in want. He makes me lie down in green pastures, he leads me beside quiet waters, he restores my soul. He guides me in paths of righteousness for his name's sake. Even though I walk through the valley of the shadow of death, I will fear no evil, for you are with me; your rod and your staff, they comfort me. You prepare a table before me in the presence of my enemies. You anoint my head with oil; my cup overflows. Surely goodness and love will follow me all the days of my life, and I will dwell in the house of the LORD forever. (Ps. 23:1-6)

The LORD is my shepherd; I have all that I need. He lets me rest in green meadows; he leads me beside peaceful streams. He renews my strength. He guides me along right paths, bringing honor to his name. Even when I walk through the darkest valley, I will not be afraid, for you are close beside me. Your rod and your staff protect and comfort me. You prepare a feast for me in the presence of my enemies. You honor me by anointing my head with oil. My cup overflows with blessings. Surely your goodness and unfailing love will pursue me all the days of my life, and I will live in the house of the LORD forever. (Ps. 23:1-6 NLT)

- ❑ Share a time when this psalm was especially meaningful to you.

- ❑ In what ways are human beings like sheep?

- ❑ What in this psalm helps you be God-secure? Write the group answers on a poster board, if one is available.

- ❑ What have you discovered in this psalm that helps you want to be God-surrendered?

THE EDGE

☐ In what ways do you feel "God-strengthened," knowing what you've discovered in this chapter?

APPLY

☐ Have fun with the group, discussing these "think-it-through" statements.

- If you love God, walk with him, and take care of yourself in appropriate ways, it is impossible for you to die one day short of the number of days God intended for you to live.

    True – False – Uncertain

- If you eat mostly junk foods, drive fast and recklessly, abuse alcohol or drugs, it is impossible for you to die one day short of the number of days God intended for you to live.

    True – False – Uncertain

☐ How have you been able to trust God in the hard things in your life? What situations have made it particularly difficult for you to trust God?

- ❑ What has led you to a point of surrender (if you have come to this point)? If not, what holds you back?

PRAY

- ❑ Begin with some quiet moments of heart examination. Pray silently, "Lord, I surrender those areas in my life where I have tried and failed."

- ❑ One at a time read the four verses below from "God's Power Pack" aloud. After each verse, pray and claim the verse for your life.

> **God's Power Pack**
> *I can do all things through him who strengthens me.*
> *Greater is he who is in me than he who is in the world.*
> *I am more than a conqueror through him who loves me.*
> *Absolutely nothing is impossible with God!*
>
> (First person paraphrase from Phil. 4:13; 1 John 4:4; Rom. 8:37; Luke 1:37)
>
> **Changing My Mind – Week 1**

Remove this verse from the back of your book and carry it with you this week. Meditate on it frequently and commit it to memory.

- ❑ Optional: if someone plays an instrument, ask that person to lead in a song of praise. Or select a song on a Christian CD and play it as the group sings along. Make certain the song isn't too difficult for group singing.

THE EDGE

SHARE

- ❑ Do you know of someone who's going through a tough time? Reach out to him or her—a caring phone call, an encouraging text or email, or get together for coffee or a meal.

- ❑ Ask God to use you to show kindness to someone this week.

- ❑ Look for an opportunity to start a conversation. When the moment is right, here are some starter questions:

  - *Have you ever had a moment when you thought you were a goner? Did someone swerve into your lane? Were you in an earthquake, tornado, or hurricane? Did you experience a frightening airline flight?*
  - *What went through your mind? How did this impact you?*

  Use your own wording. It may or may not happen, but be prepared to respond if someone turns the question back to you. You may have an opportunity to explain how God has protected your life and what your relationship with Christ means.

EXTRAS

- ❑ For insight on Psalm 23, check out the book by Phillip Keller, *A Shepherd Looks at Psalm 23* (Grand Rapids, Michigan: Zondervan Publishing House, 1970). Have someone bring a brief summary of how each phrase in Psalm 23 relates to a shepherd with his sheep.

- ❑ This is an optional discussion story if time permits. Have you ever awakened in the middle of the night with a heavy burden to pray for someone? Go to prayer immediately. You never know what may be taking place in their life. Pray for that person until God allows you to go back to sleep. Vivian Bolt, a longtime member of Woodbridge Community Church where I served as pastor, shared this story with me. Her son, Pastor Ron Bolt, confirmed the details of the story.

The Lord awakened me at 5:00 a.m. California time. I sensed that the International Interns Inc. Rezina Missions Team ministering in Moldova, a country in southeastern Europe bordered by Romania on the west and by Ukraine on the other three sides, was in serious danger. My son, Pastor Ron Bolt, was leading the short-term missions team. Not knowing anything specific, I prayed earnestly for two hours without knowing that in Moldova it was precisely 3:00 p.m. to 5:00 p.m. After praying, I felt release and peace from the Lord that everything was okay. Later I found out that at the time I was awakened, the Rezina ministry team was approaching the village of Tarosova for a 3:00 p.m. service. An angry confrontation by villagers took place that threatened an outbreak of violence. It was a time of great danger. Someone reached the mayor by cell phone, and even though he was at a major soccer event in another community, he rushed to [the group's] aid. Only the Lord knows what actual violence might have taken place had he not arrived at this very troubling scene and finally convinced the angry mob that the group had the legal right to hold the meeting. The confrontation finally settled down at 5:00 p.m. and all parties parted peacefully. The team returned the following year to Tarosova without any resistance whatsoever, and we learned authorities had communicated clearly to this village that such an incident must never be repeated."

CHAPTER TWO

WHY DID GOD DESIGN ME WITH WEAKNESSES?

A great weakness is a pretense of strength; a great strength is a humble acknowledgement of weakness.

God could easily have designed us so every year we grow stronger, better-looking, sexier, and healthier. It would have been easy for the Creator to pre-program us with steadily improving eyesight, hearing, and sense of smell while our teeth became whiter and our hair thicker. The young would aspire to get old. The old would get some respect. "Don't mess with him. He's a 125-year-old hunk, and he'll clean your clock." Just imagine having your photo taken every year to place it next to last year's photo as you congratulate yourself, *Wow, I'm getting better-looking every day.*

Obviously God designed the program to operate in reverse. Every year our physical bodies develop new aches, and something that worked fine last year now sputters. Yes, we're weak and getting weaker. Why? God is clearly up to something but before getting into the why, let's examine the four types of weaknesses: personal limitations, personal woundedness, personal sin bent, and personal weakness from the misuse of strengths.

Four Types of Weaknesses

To be successful, many think they need to impress others with their strengths and make certain no one discovers their flat side. But as strange as it sounds, admitting we're weak, frail human beings is the first step toward becoming strong. *A great weakness is a pretense of strength; a great strength is a humble acknowledgement of weakness.* The fear of appearing weak is a weakness. As you identify your weaknesses in this section, you are taking the first steps to launch God's power in a new way in your life. Let's look at the four types of weaknesses.

Type One: Personal Limitations

The majority of our weaknesses stem from the fact we're human. As a result, we have limitations in our bodies, minds, and personalities. Our mortal bodies are inherently "decaying," which means most of us face some physical issue (or issues). Some of these may be fairly minimal and sometimes humorous while others are much more difficult.

For years I lived in denial of one of my physical weaknesses, one that brought great irritation to anyone within earshot. I was a "hardcore snorer," and I tried to deny it. When confronted, I quickly shot back, "What? Me snore? I didn't hear anything, and I was there the whole night." This usually stirred a friendly argument.

Then my brother attacked my denial head-on. He recorded me one Sunday afternoon while I was flaked out on the couch. *Zzzzzz-ZZzzZz-hngggggh-Ppbhww-zZZzzzZZ.* To make matters worse, he recorded it at the end of one of our favorite musicals, *Fiddler on the Roof,* and he cranked the volume up, so it rattled the speakers. It was horrible. This was in the days of the old reel-to-reel tapes and I couldn't figure out how to erase it. So every time we played *Fiddler on the Roof,* it concluded with this hideous version of "the old man is snoring."

Denial no longer worked so I changed my tactic. I declared that people who snore in their sleep are happy. "Snoring," I argued, "is the serene vibrations of a truly contented person, somewhat like the sound of ocean waves going out and coming in." No one agreed with me but when I came downstairs in the morning and heard, "Dad, you were really happy last night," everyone laughed—and everyone knew what that meant. Eventually, I received a diagnosis of sleep apnea, and now I use a breathing mask, which eliminates snoring.

Many people live with more serious issues such as visual or hearing impairments, loss of an arm or leg, life-threatening diseases, or chronic physical pain. Daily life can be challenging and disheartening. Some impairments, such as fatigue, lupus, dyslexia, dizziness, dysfunctional internal organs, emotional illnesses, and insomnia, are not readily visible to others. The invisibility of the limitation often leads to misunderstanding and adds an extra level of stress. Other limitations may be less impairing but still embarrassing like forgetfulness, deficiencies in math, science, spelling, or grammar, being non-athletic, being directionally challenged, and so on.

When Our Weakness Torments Us

Paul's physical weakness—his thorn in the flesh—was a source of irritation, anguish, and torment.

> *To keep me from becoming conceited because of these surpassingly great revelations, there was given me a thorn in my flesh, a messenger of Satan, to torment me. Three times I pleaded with the Lord to take it away from me.* (2 Cor. 12:7-8)

Many have speculated about what Paul's thorn in the flesh was—poor eyesight, malaria, or migraine headaches are among the suggestions. The Greek word for "thorn" means a "sharp stake," and one possibility is malaria-induced headaches that may have felt like stakes being driven into his head. Others suggest Paul had poor eyesight or an eye infection since he says in his letter to the Galatians, *See what large letters I use as I write to you with my own hand!* (Gal. 6:11). However, when we consider all the possibilities, we still can't be sure.

The word used for "torment" is a Greek word that means to "beat or strike with the fist." Figuratively, Satan used Paul's thorn in the flesh to beat him up. Paul pleaded in prayer three times for his thorn in the flesh to be removed, but God's answer, using the once-for-all verb tense, was clear: *My grace is sufficient for you, for my power is made perfect in weakness* (2 Cor. 12:9). Until Paul accepted this limitation, Satan used it to discourage and defeat him. Once he was at peace with it, God uniquely displayed his power. The weakness became God's "power point"—a visual display of his power on the screen of Paul's life. This became Paul's edge, his unique advantage, to overcome adversity.

I've witnessed miraculous healings so I have no question God can supernaturally cure incurable diseases. God used Paul to heal others, but in this case, the healer wasn't healed. God used Paul's weakness in two ways: as an antidote to pride, and to amplify God's power in his life. In the book of 2 Corinthians, Paul gives an inside look into his personal journal. He includes his feelings of inadequacy, moments of despair, persecutions, and how he appropriated God's strength.

Personality Weaknesses

Different from physical limitations, personality weaknesses are those pesky character flaws each of us has whether we like to admit it or not. These shortcomings remind us that in our own strength, we are utterly weak and helpless. But in God's power, our weaknesses can become great strengths.

The Winning Edge
Extraordinary Strength
for Ordinary Weakness

Paul affirmed twice that he didn't lose heart (2 Cor. 4:1, 16). Why? With enormous obstacles, painful persecution, physical limitations, mental anguish, and bitter opponents attacking him, what kept him going? In 2 Corinthians, Paul lays bare his soul, stripping away any facade. Paul knew better than to pretend to be an all-sufficient tower of strength, a brilliant know-it-all. He often felt weak and inadequate. He leveraged every point of weakness to access the power of God. Triumphantly, he declared, *When I am weak, then I am strong.*

Paul's Weakness ... *God's Strength*

- When I am under great pressure and fearing for my life, rather than trusting in my own strength ... *I am filled with strength by trusting completely in God, who raises the dead.* (2 Cor. 1:8-9)
- When I lack confidence and feel incompetent, rather than faking it ... *I rely on God, my source for competence and confidence.* (2 Cor. 3:4-6)
- When my body is fragile as a clay pot, and I feel quite unattractive ... *I remind myself that God displays his power in my feeble body—preventing anyone from confusing God's power as coming from me.* (2 Cor. 4:7)
- When I am hard pressed by troubles ... *I am not crushed.* When I am perplexed ... *I am not in despair.* When I am persecuted ... *I am not abandoned.* When I am struck down ... *I am not destroyed.* (2 Cor. 4:8-9)
- When outwardly I feel depleted ... *I am inwardly being renewed.* (2 Cor. 4:16)
- My light and momentary troubles ... *are achieving an eternal glory.* (2 Cor. 4:17)
- Though I feel sorrow ... *I am always rejoicing.* (2 Cor. 6:10)
- *When I am poor, having little ... in Christ, I am rich, possessing everything.* (2 Cor. 6:10)

Most people who know me assume I'm a naturally organized neat-freak. Not so. This is a learned behavior. The home I grew up in was messy, a vast collection of "never-know-when-I-may-need-this" stuff. If a thief had broken into our house while we were out of town, he would have thought someone had already broken in and ransacked the place. The yard overflowed with discarded auto parts, bicycles, lawnmowers, refrigerator motors, and hundreds of other items. My dad could fix anything with a part off of something he had collected. I slept in the junk-filled basement on an army cot ignoring the sounds of dad working into the night with his power tools and the constant clatter of the rock tumbler. My dad also had about fifty to sixty junked cars he kept in a cow pasture. Now and then, he'd get suspicious someone was stealing parts from his cars. So to catch a thief, my brothers slept out there. They never caught anyone, but they considered it a high adventure. In addition, my dad visited dumps all over South Dakota to find and bring stuff home. Collecting junk and hoarding was in my DNA.

I was a sloppy, messy kid. In fifth grade, my desk must have looked like a natural disaster with stacks of papers sticking out of the desktop and piles of books and papers stashed underneath. The teacher stopped at my desk one afternoon and pointed out to the class what a mess my desk was. The embarrassment stayed with me and later inspired me to get serious about cleaning up my act.

As a teenager, I had a well-deserved reputation for being scatterbrained and forgetful. Time and time again, I'd forget an important event or school assignment. My friends tagged me "Daze" instead of "Dave." It was embarrassing. Finally, after forgetting to show for an important event and being publicly humiliated, I decided to do something about it. I purchased a calendar and notepad and began writing things down. This was the beginning of getting my life organized.

I don't function well if things get too scattered, nor do I handle multi-tasking well. I may have some natural organizational ability, but this tendency to be forgetful and scattered forces me to be organized and focused. I've leveraged my scatter-brained weakness into what most people consider a strength—being organized. This became my edge, a favorable margin, to face life's chaos.

[Joanne speaking] I struggled with shyness and timidity throughout grade school and high school and spoke very softly. My senior yearbook

THE EDGE

acknowledged this by choosing the phrase *A soft answer turns away wrath* (Prov. 15:1) to place under my picture—a nice way of saying I was very quiet.

My dad gave me the book *How to Win Friends and Influence People* by Dale Carnegie, which had a great impact on me. When I left for college at Biola, I decided with the Lord's help, I'd get out of my comfort zone and reach out to others. The opportunity came through my job in the campus cafeteria, where I recorded meal-ticket numbers. I resolved to say something kind or encouraging to each person who came through the meal line. This was a joy as I watched faces light up from my comments to them. It also landed me some dates—an unexpected perk. The experience of reaching out to encourage others changed a lot of things for me. I became comfortable putting the spotlight on others, and my confidence grew. It's how I met Dave (meal-ticket number 573), and it prepared me for my future role as a pastor's wife, leading ministries, and teaching.

Day One Time Out

Power Thoughts for Your Time Alone with God

Paul knew better than to pretend to be an all-sufficient tower of strength, a brilliant know-it-all. He often felt weak and inadequate.

❏ Read Matthew 5:3-10. To expand your thinking, the verses from the New International Version are followed by a paraphrase (version noted in parentheses).

- Blessed are the poor in spirit, for theirs is the kingdom of heaven. *You're blessed when you're at the end of your rope. With less of you there is more of God and his rule.* (MSG)

- Blessed are those who mourn, for they will be comforted. *You're blessed when you feel you've lost what is most dear to you. Only then can you be embraced by the One most dear to you.* (MSG)

- Blessed are the meek, for they will inherit the earth. *Blessed are those who are gentle, for they shall inherit the earth.* (NASB)

- Blessed are those who hunger and thirst for righteousness, for they will be filled. *You're blessed when you've worked up a good appetite for God. He's food and drink in the best meal you'll ever eat.* (MSG)

- Blessed are the merciful, for they will be shown mercy. *God blesses those people who are merciful. They will be treated with mercy!* (CEV)

- Blessed are the pure in heart, for they will see God. *You're blessed when you get your inside world—your mind and heart—put right.* (MSG)

- Blessed are the peacemakers, for they will be called sons of God. *You're blessed when you can show people how to cooperate instead of compete or fight.* (MSG)

- Blessed are those who are persecuted because of righteousness, for theirs is the kingdom of heaven. *God blesses those people who are treated badly for doing right. They belong to the kingdom of heaven.* (CEV)

> ❏ Look back over the eight beatitudes. What do you observe about how God will bless you even in weakness?
>
> ❏ Pray through the beatitudes asking God to build these character qualities in your life.
>
> ❏ Go to the back of your book and cut out or copy this week's meditation verse titled "Power Perfected in Weakness" (2 Cor. 12:9). Carry it with you and meditate on this verse throughout the week as you memorize it.

Type Two: Personal Woundedness

If you're alive and breathing, you have experienced hurts, disappointments, and personal woundedness. These are part of the package called life, and they play a role in shaping who you are. Your wounds may be related to your family and upbringing, social or economic circumstances, your personal past (including poor choices), unfair treatment, or injustice. If you're fired unjustly, you have a blemish on your employment record. Those who have a felony on their record or have served time in prison have a tough road ahead. Generally, society does not offer grace for shortcomings. Thankfully, God does. He's there for the broken, the inadequate, and the downtrodden. He offers grace that turns weaknesses into strengths, limitations into possibilities.

The apostle Paul experienced personal woundedness—physical beatings, imprisonments, shipwreck, false accusations, being deserted by co-workers, to name a few (2 Cor. 11:24-29; 2 Tim. 4:9-18). This could have pushed him over the edge to ruin and self-pity; instead, his woundedness became his cutting-edge to experience God's strength in his weakness. Rather than letting personal woundedness take him down, Paul said, *I delight in weaknesses, in insults, in hardships, in persecutions, in difficulties. For when I am weak, then I am strong* (2 Cor. 12:10).

THE EDGE

[Dave speaking] My personal story of woundedness began with growing up in an angry home. My dad's anger toward me communicated that I was unacceptable. He was a driven workaholic and demanded the same level of performance from me. To try to gain his approval, I became a driven workaholic and perfectionist. Sometimes without warning, my dad's wrath would flare, and he'd whip out his belt and come after me. If I could escape, I ran and didn't come home until the early hours of the morning. If I couldn't get away, I hunkered down in a corner trying to protect myself. Since I was often mouthy and stubborn, I honestly felt I deserved it.

I feared being around my dad not knowing when he would explode so I spent as little time at home as possible. Once when I was playing in the school band, he was upset that I was not working in his shop. He came in while the band was playing, grabbed my shirt, and pulled me from the room and down three flights of stairs to the car. I was embarrassed in front of my friends and fuming with anger. Without someone to talk with, I buried my feelings inside.

When I left home for California at age eighteen, I assumed I was leaving all that behind. My college years were a refreshing change, and I did quite well. After college and seminary, I entered the ministry. However, as the years went by, I came face to face with the unhealed issues in my life. My biggest problem was that "wherever I went, there I was."[7] I was the problem.

Some twenty years after entering the ministry, I met with a pastoral counselor. One afternoon, he asked me to tell him about my relationship with my father. I stiffened. I didn't want to talk about that subject. That was a long time ago. My father had passed away a decade earlier, and I didn't see any relevance in talking about it. But he urged me, "I think it's important for you to revisit that relationship. Take some time this week to write your memories of your relationship with your father."

Alone that week with a blank sheet of paper, I began to write my memories, and the tears flowed. I wrote page after page until I hit a buried pain, and then the tears started again. I discovered I wasn't bitter or angry with my father. More than anything else, I ached for a relationship we never had. I would have been thrilled to see him cheering in the stands even once when I played basketball, baseball, and football. When I played the lead roles in school plays, I asked him to attend, but he was too busy. He was absent for my high school graduation. I had an aching hole in my life for my father's love. I needed his approval, but never felt I was good enough to receive it. His blessing was always just out of reach, and his anger resonated in my insecurities. I came to realize that the nearly non-existent relationship with my dad was also my fault since I'd rejected him, failing to accept him as a person. I longed to reverse this, to reach out and tell him I loved him and hear him say, "I love you."

When I shared my journaling with the pastoral counselor, I was surprised when he said, "You've suffered some major trauma and damage, and it's still affecting you as a husband, father, and pastor." He helped me understand I was still acting out the learned response of cowering in the corner like the eight-year-old boy of the past. When attacked, whether as a church leader or a husband and father, I responded like a little kid hunkering down in a corner or fleeing the scene. I internalized my feelings, beat myself up, escaped, and sometimes became depressed.

I was a grown man in my forties with little-boy insecurities. The pastoral counselor worked with me to deal with my issues. What I needed was to feel accepted and valued apart from performance. I knew the theology of God's love, but I hadn't allowed it to sink deep into my sense of worth. As I began my new journey, I allowed Jesus to embrace the total me—the good, the bad, and the ugly. Knowing God had forgiven and totally accepted me reached deep into my shattered sense of worth and value. Christ's complete love and acceptance began to change my thoughts and responses when criticized or attacked.

Strength Potential in Weaknesses

Weaknesses often have a hidden strength and discovering the potential of a weakness can be life-transforming. Personal limitations, inadequacies, and woundedness can develop into strengths by accepting them and applying God's grace to them. While the following list is neither exhaustive nor absolute, it gives some exciting possibilities of what God can do.

THE EDGE

Weakness	Potential Strength
Abused	Advocate for the hurting
Anxious	Prayerful
Brokenhearted	Merciful
Daydreaming	Imaginative, creative
Depressed	Hungry for God
Difficulty sleeping	Devoted to prayer
Disadvantaged	Determined
Disabled	Compassionate
Disillusioned	Focused on the eternal
Easily offended	Sensitive to the pain of others
Exhausted	God-strengthened
Forgetful	Organized
Forsaken	Concerned for the lonely
Grieving	Comforting
Impoverished	Hard-working
Impulsive	Spontaneous
Insecure	God-confident
Intimidated	God-dependent
Outspoken	Truthful
Perfectionistic	Diligent, thorough
Physically frail	Understanding, kindhearted
Possessive	Loyal, dedicated
Quiet	Good listener
Reckless	Courageous
Rigid	Disciplined, decisive
Strong-willed	Persistent, determined
Overly sentimental	Sympathetic
Slow learner	Attentive
Wasteful	Generous, bighearted
Wounded	Compassionate, sympathetic

One of Joanne's friends tends to get overwhelmed and anxious. She's sought the Lord in prayer, meditated on Scripture relating to anxiety, and received counseling. Accepting and acknowledging her weakness has strengthened her prayer life. Recognizing that an overloaded schedule increases her level of anxiety, she prays before accepting commitments and is careful to run things by her husband before agreeing to them. She's learned to live with margins in her life, allowing enough time for each activity or event. She practices daily balance—sleep, exercise, healthy eating, meditation, and prayer. Her life exemplifies leveraging a weakness to become a stronger person.

Type Three: Personal Sin Bent

Stubbornness. An explosive temper. Addictive behavior. Uncontrolled lust. Self-centeredness. A judgmental or critical spirit. We can't escape this third form of weakness. It's called the sin nature, and we all have one. The apostle Paul struggled with his sin nature. *I do not understand what I do. For what I want to do I do not do, but what I hate I do* (Rom. 7:15). He adds his self-assessment of the turmoil within. *I know that nothing good lives in me, that is, in my sinful nature. For I have the desire to do what is good, but I cannot carry it out* (Rom. 7:18).

I've wondered why Paul didn't name the sin that caused him such great frustration. In all likelihood, it was too personal, perhaps embarrassing. I also think his many critics and foes could have used it against him. It's my hunch Paul's close companions knew the details and prayed for him in his struggle. The same may be true for you. There may be a sin weakness that isn't appropriate for you to broadcast to everyone, everywhere. Instead, confide in a close friend who understands and will be your prayer partner and hold you accountable.

Everyone has a unique vulnerability, an area where they're most susceptible. Some are wired with a hot temper and easily explode while others are so laid-back that blowing off steam isn't an issue. One person may struggle with addiction while another person has no desire for addictive substances but is prone to jealousy. Others struggle with lust and pornography while this isn't a temptation for someone else. Whatever it may be, your enemy knows it and targets you at your point of greatest vulnerability.

Our bents aren't necessarily sinful, but they may lead us into sin. Messiness—leaving the pizza box, chicken wings, socks, shoes, and newspaper strewn around the family room—isn't sinful *per se*. However, if this is an area of contention with your spouse, your response of insensitivity and stubbornness *is* sinful. Watching a football game isn't sin, but watching football for nineteen hours over Thanksgiving weekend while neglecting time with God and family and shirking

THE EDGE

household duties is both a weakness and wrong.

We all come pre-designed with a sin bent, a tendency toward weakness. Which of the following do you struggle with? We'll discuss how to deal with these later in the chapter.

Common Sin Bents and Behaviors

Abusing others	Drunkenness	Quarreling, disputing
Abusing yourself	Gluttony	Rebellious
Addictive behavior	Gossipy, nosy	Rude, insensitive
Blaming, fault-finding	Greedy, stingy	Resentful, bitter
Complaining, whining	Lustful, immoral	Selfish ambition
Conceited, self-important	Independent spirit	Sexual immorality
Conniving, devious	Jealousy, envy	Substance abuse
Controlling, nagging	Manipulating, using others	Swearing, profanity
Critical, cutting	Materialism, idolatry	Uncontrolled temper
Deceitful, fraudulent	Needing to always be right	Violent behavior
Demanding	Occult activity	
Divisive, contentious	Pornography	

Sin leaves a trail of destruction, and it also distorts our thinking. I grew up looking into a distorted mirror—like a strange carnival mirror with a twisted picture—seeing my faults and flaws magnified and distorted. I acted out what I saw in the mirror. With God's forgiveness of my sins and by his grace, I began to look into a new mirror and learn healthier ways of thinking. Knowing God forgave me and totally accepted me reached deep into my shattered sense of worth and value. Christ's complete love and acceptance began to change my thoughts and responses. The new mirror reflecting these qualities began to change how I saw myself.

- I am loved and accepted, completely and unconditionally (Isa. 54:10; Eph. 2:4; Rom. 15:7).
- I am forgiven, fully and repeatedly (Isa. 43:25; 1 John 1:9).
- I am blameless, without fault in God's presence (Eph. 1:4).
- I am God-designed, intricately and marvelously created (Ps. 139:13-14).
- I am valued, my life has meaning and purpose (1 Pet. 5:7; Ps. 138:8).

I wrote these five qualities on a notecard and began carrying them with me. These truths began to change my sense of worth and value.

Day Two Time Out

Power Thoughts for Your Time Alone with God
Knowing God forgave me and totally accepted me reached deep into my shattered sense of worth and value.

- ❏ Marvel as you read and reflect on God's love in Ephesians 1:3-14.

- ❏ Of the five phrases ("I am loved and accepted, forgiven, blameless, God-designed, and valued"), which one is the hardest for you to believe? Which ones help you the most with your sin bents?

- ❏ As you pray, reflect on these five statements and thank God for his overwhelming love. Write them on a card and carry them with you.

    I am loved, completely and unconditionally.

    I am forgiven, fully and repeatedly.

    I am blameless, without fault in God's presence.

    I am God-designed, intricately and marvelously created.

    I am valued; my life has meaning and purpose.

Type Four: Personal Weakness Disguised as a Strength

At first glance, this type of weakness may seem perplexing. How can strengths be weaknesses? Does this diminish the value of strengths? Strengths, generally speaking, are a positive, but like any good gift, they can be misused or neglected. As weaknesses have positive potential, strengths also have the potential to be weaknesses. Before getting into potential misuse, let's begin with a brief look at strengths and gifts.

Knowing Your Strengths and Gifts

God designed everyone with a unique combination of strengths and weaknesses. While the focus of this chapter is on God's power being perfected in weakness, it's important not to overlook the flipside to the subject—your strengths. Discovering and engaging your strengths is important, and I recommend STRENGTHS FINDER, the popular Gallup assessment to detect your natural abilities and aptitudes.[8] STRENGTHS FINDER is available in twenty languages and has been used by more than ten million people in one hundred nations. The tool is a brief assessment and once completed, you'll receive a profile indicating your five areas of greatest aptitude. Examples of the assessment's talent themes include achiever, analytical, connectedness, consistency, empathy, futuristic, learner, and strategic to name a few of the thirty-four aptitudes.

As a believer, you've also been given a spiritual gift or gifts (usually more than one). These are different than natural strengths, but the two often work hand in hand. The New Testament has much to stay about spiritual gifts, but in brief, here are two important points. First: be knowledgeable about your spiritual gifts. Paul wrote, *Now about spiritual gifts, brothers, I do not want you to be ignorant* (1 Cor. 12:1). For a list of spiritual gifts, see Romans 12:6-8, Ephesians 4:11-12, 1 Corinthians 12:8-10, 28, and 1 Peter 4:9-11. Second: do not neglect to exercise your spiritual gifts. Peter wrote, *Each of you has been blessed with one of God's many wonderful gifts to be used in the service of others. So use your gift well* (1 Pet. 4:10 CEV). You may find it helpful to ask a mature believer to help you discover your gifts and how God can use you in exercising them.

Our natural strengths and spiritual gifts are from God. Think of them as treasures—in a positive manner as resources to bless others, or negatively as sources of false pride. For the moment, let's compare your "strengths-gifts treasure" with "financial treasure." Money can be a great blessing to help others, or it can be a source of pride, hoarding, and self-sufficiency. Money itself isn't the problem—it's having a twisted attitude about money that creates the problem (1 Tim. 6:10). As money can be misused so can your strengths and spiritual gifts.

Preventing Over-confidence

Paul was a multi-talented, highly educated, fiercely driven achiever before coming to Christ. As he said, *If anyone else thinks he has reasons to put confidence in the flesh, I have more* (Phil. 3:4). Paul rose to the top; he was the best of the best. If he were in the military, he'd be a Navy Seal or a Green Beret. If he were in business, he'd be the CEO of a Fortune 500 company. Over-confidence was a real and present danger to Paul because of his background, education, and high level of achievement. To prevent himself from being over-confident, Paul put no confidence in the flesh (Phil. 3:3).

As mentioned earlier, weaknesses have positive potential, and strengths have the potential to be a weakness. Those with a high intellect may find they can coast and get good grades. By failing to achieve their potential, their strength becomes a weakness. The same can be said for those with exceptional athletic ability or a charming personality. Their strength allows them to slide by, and this tendency then becomes a weakness.

Several times I've asked an audience for a show of hands. "How many received honors as an athlete? How many were cheerleaders? Were any of you class presidents or a homecoming king or queen? How many received music or art awards or were honor students? How many have masters or doctorate degrees?" Hands go up, and I sincerely congratulate them on their achievements. I then point out these two verses as an encouragement to the large number of people who didn't raise their hand.

> *I don't see many of "the brightest and the best" among you, not many influential, not many from high-society families. Isn't it obvious that God deliberately chose men*

and women that the culture overlooks and exploits and abuses? (1 Cor. 1:26-27 MSG)

If you've received honors and awards, this doesn't mean God can't use you. On the contrary, he'll use you greatly but sometimes it takes a little longer. Why? God has to get you past relying on your accolades and awards.[9] Multi-talented believers may subtly congratulate themselves: *God, you're really fortunate to have me on your side. After all, I was an All-State basketball player, honor student, president of my class, and voted most likely to succeed.* And then God allows them to flounder and face one defeat after another. Why? God must bring them to the end of themselves. They must get acquainted with their weaknesses to experience God's power. After they're broken and have learned humility, God will use them greatly—but not until then.

Through the years, I've known a number of leaders with winsome personalities and exceptional speaking abilities. Relying on their natural gifts and with little preparation, they can get up in front of an audience and "wing it." Their strength becomes a weakness in two ways. They could be much more effective with preparation, and their pride stands in the way of their being greatly used by God. Subtly, they draw attention to themselves. Paul David Tripp says they become "very skilled self-swindlers."[10] I've also watched God set aside some of these highly gifted individuals—sometimes through failure—so they'd come to the end of themselves and start relying totally on Christ.

Surprisingly, Paul says this about his impeccable credentials:

> *But whatever was to my profit I now consider loss for the sake of Christ. What is more, I consider everything a loss compared to the surpassing greatness of knowing Christ Jesus my Lord, for whose sake I have lost all things. I consider them rubbish that I may gain Christ.* (Phil. 3:7-8)

The word he uses for "rubbish" refers to trash, or more specifically, dung—cow manure. Paraphrased, Paul says, *The very credentials these people are waving around as something special, I'm tearing up and throwing out with the trash—along with everything else I used to take credit for* (Phil. 3:7 MSG).

THE EDGE

Some assume Paul jumped up from his conversion on the Damascus Road and launched his first missionary journey. Not so. After surrendering his life to Christ, Paul spent three years in the desert of Arabia (Gal. 1:16-18), followed by eleven years serving Christ in relative obscurity. If Paul was thirty years of age when he came to Christ (which is likely, considering his training and accomplishments as a Pharisee), he didn't launch his first missionary journey until he was forty-four or forty-five years of age.

John Darby, a spiritual leader and Bible translator from the 1800s, said, "It is God's way to set people aside after their first start that self-confidence may die down. ... We must get to know ourselves and that we have no strength."[11] This was the case for Paul and it was also true for Moses, who served forty years in Pharaoh's court followed by forty years tending sheep and getting his BD degree (Backside of the Desert degree). He was eighty years old when he began leading the children of Israel through the wilderness.

Often God "sets us aside" to give us time to understand our weaknesses and learn to serve in the power of the Spirit rather than the flesh. The antidote to "self-swindling" is to abandon our parade of self-righteousness and daily admit our life is a mess without continuous forgiveness, grace, and transformation.

If you're prone to charge ahead, relying on your natural abilities, keep serving—but slow down to recognize your weaknesses and acknowledge that you have no strength in yourself. Learn to wait on God. Listen to God and God's people. Learn to value others. Allow your pride and stubbornness to be broken. Humble yourself before the Lord. *Get down on your knees before the Master; it's the only way you'll get on your feet* (James 4:10 MSG).

Day Three Time Out

Power Thoughts for Your Time Alone with God
"It is God's way to set people aside after their first start that their self-confidence may die down. ... We must learn to know ourselves and that we have no strength." John Darby

❑ Read 1 Corinthians 1:25-31.

❑ What have been your proudest achievements? What honors have you received? In what ways have these helped or hindered you?

❑ As you seek God in prayer, ask him to show you the difference between pride and humility.

When I'm proud, I'm confident in how much I know. When I'm humble, I'm aware of how much I have to learn.

When I'm proud, I harbor resentments and deny their effect on my attitude. When I'm humble, I choose to forgive others as Christ has forgiven me.

When I'm proud, I trust in myself. When I'm humble, I trust in God, knowing I'll certainly fail without his leading.

When I'm proud, I'm certain I don't need to change. When I'm humble, I daily admit my need for grace, forgiveness, and transformation.

Now add a few of your own ...

Why Weaknesses?

Most people have all four types of weaknesses, so don't assume you're the only one. In fact, Paul had all four types: 1) personal limitations—his thorn in the flesh; 2) personal woundedness—he got beat up a lot by his enemies, verbally and physically; 3) personal sin bent—he agonized over his sin bent in Romans 7; and 4) personal strengths that could have been his weaknesses had he relied on them.

To get a clear picture of why God designed us with weaknesses, let's focus on the classic verses on this topic.

> *To keep me from becoming conceited because of these surpassingly great revelations, there was given me a thorn in my flesh, a messenger of Satan, to torment me. Three times I pleaded with the Lord to take it away from me. But he said to me, "My grace is sufficient for you, for my power is made perfect in weakness." Therefore I will boast all the more gladly about my weaknesses, so that Christ's power may rest on me. That is why, for Christ's sake, I delight in weaknesses, in insults, in hardships, in persecutions, in difficulties. For when I am weak, then I am strong.* (2 Cor. 12:7-10)

In this passage, we discover answers to why God designed us with weaknesses and how he's using them to accomplish his purposes.

1. Weaknesses keep you humble.

Have you been around people who think they're "perfection personified"? They put on a show of how smart, healthy, successful, and wealthy they are, subtly implying it's too bad you can't be flawless too. It's nauseating and phony. The Bible says, *First pride, then the crash—the bigger the ego, the harder the fall* (Prov. 16:18 MSG). In fact, I find it difficult to think of any sin that doesn't have pride at the root.

Instead, God wants us to have a proper perspective of ourselves. Paul used the phrase *to keep me from becoming conceited* (2 Cor. 12:7).

THE EDGE

Because of the astounding revelations he had in the third heaven (2 Cor. 12:1-7), God used this "thorn in the flesh" to keep him humble.

Weaknesses are not about having a dinged-up self-image. God gives us incredible resources for a strong sense of worth: we're children of God; we're holy and blameless because of Christ; we have a personal friendship with the Creator. Now, so we don't waltz around thinking we're "little gods," God supplies us with a first-class set of weaknesses. As Romans 12:3 says, *Don't cherish exaggerated ideas of yourself or your importance, but try to have a sane estimate of your capabilities* (Phillips NT).

2. God uses weaknesses to bring you to the end of yourself.

God encouraged Paul with these amazing words: *My grace is sufficient for you, for my power is made perfect in weakness* (2 Cor. 12:9). The word "sufficient" (Greek word *arkeo*) means "to be satisfied, to be content." This is the same word translated "to be content" in Philippians 4:11-12. Paul never said, "I am content in whatever state I am in because I am a naturally contented person." No one is naturally contented. Instead, he said, *I have learned to be content,* and *I have learned the secret of being filled and going hungry* (Phil. 4:11-12 NASB).

Contentment is not learned when you have a ton of money and great success. You only want more. You'll never be able to fine-tune your life to achieve perfect contentment. Contentment is learned when you're exhausted, depleted—at your rope's end. You discover contentment when you come to the end of yourself. It is in these moments, when life turns difficult, that you discover the only source for contentment: JESUS PLUS NOTHING. He is sufficient; he is all you need. Then, as we grow in Christ-centered contentment, we discover *godliness with contentment is great gain*, and God *richly provides us with everything for our enjoyment* (1 Tim. 6:6, 17).

Jamin Goggin, writing with Kyle Strobel in *Beloved Dust*, describes when his whole world came crashing down.[12]

> I was a tornado of frailty, insecurity, and shame. ... Then the strategies of managing and avoiding my situation were stripped away. Within that place of chaos, I began to hear the call of God and the truth he had for me. He

was teaching me the truth of my identity—that I was limited, needy, and feeble. Ultimately, I could not control my world. All my best efforts could not guarantee me anything. I was not master of *my* universe, let alone *the* universe. He was teaching me that I am a creature and he is the Creator. He was teaching me that I am dust.

God's grace is sufficient, and it is also extravagant. As Jack Miller said, "Cheer up! You're a worse sinner than you ever dared imagine, and you're more loved than you ever dared hope."[13] God's grace is forgiveness for your most grievous sin and sufficiency for your most difficult limitation. God's grace heals your personal woundedness, and his grace empowers you to forgive. The Christian life is grace upon grace and more grace … until we become grace-giving and gracious people. God's grace saves you, and his grace shapes you.

3. Weaknesses and brokenness give you a power-edge to be used by God.

Look back again at 2 Corinthians 12:9-10. The words "weak, weakness, weaknesses" appear four times. This is the Greek word *astheneia*, a general word in the Bible for sickness, illness, or a lack of strength. *Asthenia* is a medical word in use today, meaning "the lack or loss of strength or energy, a sense of fatigue, or muscle weakness." In the field of psychiatry, *asthenia* refers to a lack of dynamic force in the personality or a fear of effort.[14]

In a general sense, *asthenia* indicates a lack of strength, an inability to cope with life. Life's trials and troubles seem overwhelming. The frailty of *astheneia* may be physical, emotional, or mental.

Compare the word "weakness" with the word "power" or "strength," used three times in verses 9 and 10. The word "power" is the Greek word *dunamis* from which we derive the English word "dynamite" or "dynamic." As direct opposites, "weakness" is in sharp contrast to "power"—like comparing the fizz in a soda to the explosive power of dynamite.

Let's connect the two words—"weakness" and "power." God made the earth and flung galaxies into place, and he created the mighty oceans and mountains. Nothing is greater than God's power. But how is this mighty power of God perfected? In verse 9, God says, *My power [Greek dunamis] is perfected in weakness [Greek astheneia]*. The word "perfected" is the Greek word *teleios* (source of English words like telescope, telephone, television, telegenic, etc.), meaning "to bring something to completion, to fulfill an ultimate purpose." Here's the key: *God's awesome power, the power that creates and sustains the universe, is brought to its culmination, a crowning crescendo, a triumphant exclamation—in your daily weaknesses*. Wow!

4. God uses weaknesses to get you ready for the main event.

It's difficult to wrap our minds around this, but this life is not the main event. "You only go around once, so get all the gusto you can" is the attitude that permeates the thinking of most people. But that's faulty thinking. The main event is eternity and this life is preparation for "forever and forever." If we got healthier and stronger and better-looking every year, we'd never want to leave this life. Instead, as our bodies decline, God is preparing us to spend eternity with him in perfect, glorified bodies. Coming to terms with our weaknesses gives us an edge to live for the eternal. The Bible says this about the death of our human body: *It is sown in weakness, it is raised in power; it is sown a natural body, it is raised a spiritual body* (1 Cor. 15:43-44). I'm ready for my new body ... and the sooner, the better! How about you?

Day Four Time Out

Power Thoughts for Your Time Alone with God
God's awesome power—the power that creates and sustains the universe—is brought to its culmination, a crowning crescendo, a triumphant exclamation—in your daily weaknesses.

❑ Read 2 Corinthians 12:7-10 from your Bible and then compare it to this paraphrase from *The Message*.

Because of the extravagance of those revelations, and so I wouldn't get a big head, I was given the gift of a handicap to keep me in constant touch with my limitations. Satan's angel did his best to get me down; what he in fact did was push me to my knees. No danger then of walking around high and mighty! At first I didn't think of it as a gift, and begged God to remove it. Three times I did that, and then he told me, "My grace is enough; it's all you need. My strength comes into its own in your weakness." Once I heard that, I was glad to let it happen. I quit focusing on the handicap and began appreciating the gift. It was a case of Christ's strength moving in on my weakness. Now I take limitations in stride, and with good cheer, these limitations that cut me down to size—abuse, accidents, opposition, bad breaks. I just let Christ take over! And so the weaker I get, the stronger I become. (2 Cor. 12:7-10 MSG)

❑ What weaknesses have been discouraging and difficult for you? In what ways have your weaknesses pushed you to your knees, so you don't walk around high and mighty?

❑ Ask God what he wants to accomplish in your life through your weaknesses.

How to Turn Weakness to Strength

God's plan is to perfect his power in your weakness, so here's how to get started on your lifelong journey of turning weakness into strength.

1. Accept your weaknesses.

Paul said *I delight in weaknesses* (2 Cor. 12:10). Was he being masochistic? No. "Paul took no pleasure in the pain itself but rejoiced in the power of Christ that it revealed through him."[15] God knows your weaknesses better than you do, and he has either designed them in your DNA or allowed them through your life experiences. God has been involved throughout the entire process. Even if you suffer deep scars from living in sin, God knows this, and he is ready to turn ashes into beauty. Now is the moment to take action: move from self-rejection and embarrassment at your weaknesses to accepting them. Take the time right now to pray:

> Thank you, Lord, for my personal limitations, woundedness, and sin bents. This is difficult to do because I have often wished I didn't have these things in my life, but now I realize you designed me this way, and you were overseeing each event in my life. I choose to accept these weaknesses, knowing you will display your power through them.

2. Play dead ... because you *are* dead.

Regarding your sin bent, acknowledge that you're powerless to change your sin nature and its destructive, deceitful, arrogant ways. Realize God uses spiritual frustration and failure to turn you from trusting yourself to trusting in him. Your sin nature cannot be controlled, reformed, or improved by the noblest effort of human will-power.

When your sin nature is tantalized by a juicy temptation, play dead—because you *are* dead. *For you died, and your life is now hidden with Christ in God. ... Put to death, therefore, whatever belongs to your earthly nature: sexual immorality, impurity, lust, evil desires and greed, which is idolatry* (Col. 3:3, 5).

Carey is a believer who struggles with alcohol. His health is severely threatened, and he'll probably die from the effects of alcohol if he doesn't stop. Numerous times he's tried to have just one beer, but that stokes the fire for more. Eight to ten beers later, he's drunk and doing stupid things. He's aware of his sin and knows he needs to do something about it. Here's the advice I gave to him:

"Sam, before you die, you have to die."

"What?"

"Yes. The only solution to your problem with alcohol is to die to alcohol's power. Sam, have you ever met a dead person who's still dying for a drink?"

"No, I guess not."

"Does the desire for alcohol end at the point of death?"

"I haven't experienced that, but I reckon it does."

"So, Sam, this is what God wants you to do. Play dead because you *are* dead. When the temptation comes—and it will—rather than putting up a big fight to not have a drink, claim your position in Christ. Visualize yourself hanging on the cross, limp, lifeless, unresponsive. Hide yourself in Christ and reckon yourself to be dead. The temptation has no power over you when you claim your position in Christ."

In addition, I urged him to participate in a recovery group and have a sponsor to check in with daily.

This is God's method to overcome the sin nature, and it works because it's the power of the cross. Paul exclaimed, *May I never boast except in the cross of our Lord Jesus Christ, through which the world has been crucified to me, and I to the world* (Gal. 6:14). To boast in the cross is to *be* on the cross, crucified with Christ, and *always carry around in our body the death of Jesus, so that the life of Jesus may also be revealed in our body* (2 Cor. 4:10). "Boasting in the cross" is essentially the same as "boasting in weakness," the next point.

3. Boast about your weaknesses.

I admit this sounds strange. What did Paul mean when he said, *I will boast all the more gladly about my weaknesses, so that Christ's power may rest on me* (2 Cor. 12:9)?

Boasting about your weakness is not whining and complaining. This isn't an excuse to rehearse your aches and pains over and over again to the irritation of all who hear you. It isn't a martyr complex attempting to draw attention to yourself and your noble sacrifices.

Boasting about your weakness does not prohibit speaking of your accomplishments or credentials when appropriate. There is a danger of becoming a self-effacing person with a phony humility. When Paul confronted the boisterous, bragging false teachers, he went head-to-head with quite a list of his credentials and what he had gone through for the sake of Christ (2 Cor. 11:16-29). He concluded by saying, *If I must boast, I will boast of the things that show my weakness* (11:30). In the next chapter, Paul describes his experience of being caught up into paradise to receive direct revelation from God (2 Cor. 12:1-6). He follows this incredible credential with these words to the Corinthians:

> *I ought to have been commended by you, for I am not in the least inferior to the "super-apostles," even though I am nothing. The things that mark an apostle—signs, wonders and miracles—were done among you with great perseverance.* (2 Cor. 12:11-12)

There is a time to mention accomplishments and credentials but not for the purpose of boasting. The bottom line is this: HE WHO BOASTS IS TO BOAST IN THE LORD. *For it is not he who commends himself that is approved, but he whom the Lord commends* (2 Cor. 10:17-18 NASB).

Boasting about your weakness is an attitude of thankfulness, not complaining. The weakness may be painful, perhaps the biggest trial of your life. Boasting about your weakness is giving thanks *in* all your circumstances (1 Thess. 5:18), not *for* all your circumstances. No one in their right mind is thankful they have cancer. But you can be thankful for God's grace giving you sustaining strength as you deal with cancer.

Boasting about your weakness is a willingness to be real, authentic. Pretending to be invincible is a great weakness; acknowledging weakness is a first step toward great strength. We may reason to ourselves, *I don't want others to know I'm struggling with this weakness. What will they think of me?* To prevent others from getting too close, we build a wall of independence and self-reliance. "Acknowledging weaknesses not only draws a person closer to God; it draws the person closer to other people. Weakness is the great leveler."[16]

One of my weaknesses is over-eating. I admire people who can eat just two cookies. I start out with a baker's dozen. Some people are on a gluten-free diet, but I'm still working on a gluttony-free diet. I have a weakness for food—particularly if it's free. When I acknowledge my weakness and ask others to pray for me, I'm strengthened. This is an "advantageous-edge" to keep from going over a "dangerous-edge." My small group knows my weakness and helps keep me accountable.

Boasting about your weakness shines the spotlight on Jesus. Paul said he boasts about his weaknesses *so that Christ's power may rest on me* (2 Cor. 12:9). This phrase means Christ's power will be "a tent or a shelter" over you. Live in the tent of Christ's power over you. For example, if someone commends you for your restraint in choosing fruit when an entire array of desserts is available, your comment can be, "Thank you. It's possible only through Christ's power over me. I'm capable of making myself sick from overeating."

4. Allow God to display his power through your weaknesses.

Who better to minister to someone with the loss of a limb, childhood abuse, unemployment, addiction, rejection, or loneliness than someone who's gone through the same experience? Out of your deepest hurt will come your greatest opportunity to help others. Paul said, *Who is weak without my feeling that weakness?* (2 Cor. 11:29 NLT). In your weakness, you'll have the opportunity to touch more lives than you ever imagined. God said, *My power works best in weakness,* and Paul affirmed it: *When I am weak, then I am strong* (2 Cor. 12:9-10).

When Don Klassen, Joanne's cousin, was six years old, someone threw a bamboo stick that hit him in the left eye. His eye popped out of the socket and lay dangling on his cheek. Surgeons attempted to rescue the eye, but eventually they had to replace it with a glass eye (a plastic eye now). In Don's sensitive, formative years growing up, kids made fun of his glass eye, and girls said they couldn't handle being with someone with only one eye. Embarrassed, he had difficulty talking about his disability. Once he accepted his weakness, however, God began to use it in amazing ways. To overcome his lack of confidence, Don received training in public speaking. Today Don, married with three children and nine grandchildren, has had a unique ministry for several decades helping boys overcome their feelings of rejection. He is often asked to share his story with men's groups. God's power is magnified through a plastic eye and a humble man willing to tell his story.

Value in an Old Lamp

While in junior high school woodshop, I made a lamp in the shape of a pump. Years later, I found it in storage. The wiring was frayed, the handle was broken, and the finish was scratched and defaced. My first thought was to dump it, but just before tossing it, my mind drifted back to woodshop and how proud I was when I brought that lamp home. Though it looked like a piece of junk, the value of that lamp was rekindled in my mind. I began to picture it repaired and refinished. In my spare time, I began working on that lamp—sanding, repairing, refinishing, and rewiring it. Today it's a treasured keepsake on my bedroom dresser.

The lamp didn't change itself. It only cooperated with the process. If the lamp jumped off the dresser and started talking—"Don't I look good? I did a pretty good job fixing myself up"— after I laughed myself silly and picked myself up off the floor, I'd be upset with the lamp's arrogance. Don't assume you're the one turning weakness into strength. God does the sanding, polishing, refinishing, and rewiring, and he is the power source.

I'm like that lamp, one toss away from the trash—faulty wiring, scarred finish, broken handle. And yet God values me. I'm his workmanship. He's patiently sanding, refinishing, rewiring, and changing me to reflect his light.

God made me, sin marred me, and Christ is mending me—from weakness to strength.

Day Five Time Out

Power Thoughts for Your Time Alone with God
Realize that God uses spiritual frustration and failure to turn you from trusting yourself to trusting in him.

- ❑ Read Colossians 3:1-10.

- ❑ Think about the last time you experienced spiritual frustration or failure. How did you respond? What was God teaching you?

- ❑ Have you tried "playing dead because you *are* dead" when you face temptation? Put this into practice this week when temptation comes knocking.

STRENGTH TEAM

SESSION TWO

WHY DID GOD DESIGN ME WITH WEAKNESSES?

Is it a surprise that God's power works best when we're weak? Most Christians would like to experience more of God's power but have never seriously considered Paul's statement: *When I am weak, then I am strong* (2 Cor. 12:9). Let's get ready for an exciting session of discovering why God designed us with weaknesses and how he perfects his power in our weakness.

CONNECT

- Share a time when you felt particularly weak either physically, emotionally, or spiritually. What did you learn from that experience?

GROW

- Ask members of the group to read these passages aloud: 2 Corinthians 12:7-10, 2 Timothy 4:14-18, Romans 7:15-19, and Philippians 3:4-10. Pause after each passage to identify the weakness type and discuss examples, so everyone understands what's meant. Allow time for each person to identify one or more weaknesses in each area and share it if they're comfortable doing so.

    1) Personal limitation: _____

    2) Personal woundedness: _____

    3) Personal sin bent: _____

    4) Personal weakness from a misused strength: _____

- Discuss these two statements and how you've seen them to be true in your life.

THE EDGE

So I wouldn't get a big head, I was given the gift of a handicap to keep me in constant touch with my limitations. Satan's angel did his best to get me down; what he in fact did was push me to my knees. No danger then of walking around high and mighty! (2 Cor. 12:7 MSG)

Until Paul accepted this limitation, Satan used it to discourage and defeat him. Once he was at peace with it, God uniquely displayed his power. The weakness became God's 'power point'—a visual display of his power on the screen of Paul's life.

APPLY

❏ Discuss how you would apply these four steps to turn your weakness into strength.
  1. Accept your weaknesses
  2. Play dead because you *are* dead
  3. Boast about your weaknesses (practice what you'd say about one of your weaknesses)
  4. Allow God's power to be displayed through your weaknesses

❏ Read aloud in unison the "Changing My Mind" verse for this week.

Power Perfected in Weakness

"My grace is sufficient for you, for my power is made perfect in weakness." Therefore I will boast all the more gladly about my weaknesses, so that Christ's power may rest on me. (2 Cor. 12:9 NIV)

Changing My Mind - Week 2

PRAY

❏ Give everyone a paper clip. In silence, unfold the paper clip, symbolizing the yielding of your personal limitations, woundedness, sin bents, and strengths to God. Then form the clip into a heart, symbolizing God's plan to take your weaknesses and make you strong for his glory. Hold the heart in your hand as the leader prays.

Prayer: "God, we thank you that we can come to you. You designed us with weaknesses and have allowed the experiences of life that have shaped us. We surrender our false sense of strength to you and admit how frail, weak, and needy we really are. Thank you for your acceptance, forgiveness, and your unconditional love. Like these paper clips, shape us into people who are strong, pliable, and usable for your kingdom, Amen."

- ❏ Optional: close with a song of worship (use a CD to sing with or have someone lead with an instrument).

SHARE

- ❏ This week, be alert to people you meet who are exhausted, discouraged, or frustrated. Look for an opportunity to share an encouraging word or listen to them with compassion.

- ❏ Here are some thought-provoking questions that may ignite a discussion of God's strength and human weakness:

- *What is the toughest challenge you've ever faced? How did you handle it? Did you feel strong or weak when you faced this?*

- *Where do you find strength when you're exhausted or feel hopeless?*

- *What do you think of the statement "When I am weak, then I am strong"?*

CHAPTER THREE
CHANGING MY MIND

*Since your mind controls your behavior,
let God control your mind and your behavior will change.*

Our memory (or lack of it) makes for great humor. You've likely heard, "You no sooner get your face cleared up than your memory goes." Or, "The mind is a wonderful thing. It starts working the minute you're born and never stops until you get up to speak in public." Some joker said, "I'm not suffering from insanity. I'm enjoying every minute of it." In jest, I tell people who meet with me, "You can share your darkest secrets in absolute confidence--at my age, I probably won't remember what you said by morning." Humor aside, our brains are amazing beyond comprehension.

During the 1956 US presidential campaign, a woman called out to candidate Adlai E. Stevenson, "Senator, you have the vote of every thinking person!" Stevenson shouted back, "That's not enough, madam, we need a majority!"[17] He had a great point: serious thinking about what we think and how it affects our lives is rare. Let's break out of that rut and do some serious thinking about thinking.

Transforming the mind is essential to turning weaknesses into strengths. Memories, life experiences, and feelings affect our mental attitudes and behaviors. Sometimes bad memories play havoc with our thought life and leave us with weaknesses that sideline us. Even as a

Christian, you may feel victimized and helpless, with negative thought patterns you can't shake. When you became a Christian, you received cleansing and forgiveness of your sins and a new life in Christ. But God doesn't hit FORMAT to delete all the gunk from your mental hard drive.

Is it possible to transform and heal the inner thoughts of the human mind? Millions worldwide are gripped with agonizing mental images that control their lives every minute of the day. Is it possible to break these chains of mental bondage?

- Scarring memories of a tragic accident
- Post-traumatic stress from war
- Shattered personal worth and lack of confidence
- Controlling compulsions and obsessions
- Attitudes of gloom, cynicism, and suicidal thoughts
- Memories of hundreds or perhaps thousands of pornographic images
- Scarring mental or physical abuse
- Memories of a past promiscuous lifestyle
- Uncontrollable fears and phobias

Tackling these issues is a tall order, but God promises the human mind can be renewed—literally transformed from the inside out. God has given you his Word and the power of the Holy Spirit to take on this task. Like a virus scanner or defragmenter in a computer, he searches your mind to find and correct the areas that weaken your Christian faith. *Since your mind controls your behavior, let God control your mind and your behavior will change.* The process is amazing and supernatural, but not automatic. It requires an investment on your part.

Before digging into the "how to" for transforming the mind, let's start with an overview of current research regarding the wonders and astounding capacity of your mind. This information is crucial to better understand the process of transforming the mind.

THE EDGE

Your Neck-top Computer

Your mind is a powerhouse of potential, one of the most complex objects in the known universe. Though the brain is little more than the size of a large grapefruit, its capacity and versatility far surpasses any computer in the world. This "God-designed neck-top computer" weighs in at about three pounds.

The component parts of your mind are staggering: "It is estimated that the brain contains more than one hundred billion nerve cells, which is about the number of stars in the Milky Way. Each nerve cell is connected to other nerve cells by thousands of individual connections between cells."[18] Some 100,000 miles of nerve fibers connect the various components of the mind.[19] In addition, the one hundred billion nerve cells, or neurons, connect with each other up to 60,000 times. And to think all this fits into a size-seven hat![20] The signals of the brain are passed along at speeds up to 268 miles per hour. After each signal passes, it takes the filament about 1/2000 of a second to chemically recharge itself. At each firing, one nerve chemically communicates with another.[21]

If every person on the planet simultaneously made 200,000 phone calls, this would be the same total number of connections of the human brain in a single day.[22] Wow! *Fearfully and wonderfully made* the Psalmist David exclaimed in astonishment at God's creation of the human mind and body (Ps. 139:14).

If family and friends chide you for having a one-track mind, take heart. They're wrong. You have two-tracks or two hemispheres in your brain, and you use both. "On the left, you have the talker, reader, speaker, writer, all-around deep-thinker. On the right, you'll find that music-lover, the deep-dreamer, the artsy type."[23] The left side is the analyzing, organizing, conceptual think-tank while the right brain specializes in feeling, touching, and empathy. The dominant side for most men is the left side while for women it's the right. However, everyone uses both the right and left sides of the brain, and both are continually in play.

A dense bundle of nerves known as the *corpus callosum* serves to connect your brain's right and left hemispheres. And a lively connection it is, with each of the 200-million nerve fibers in the corpus callosom firing a nerve impulse twenty times a second. Right now, 4 billion impulses are playing a game of high-speed ping-pong between your ears.[24] Next time you can't make it to work because of a throbbing headache, just tell your boss you're suffering from a corpus callosum right brain, left brain, high-speed ping-pong headache involving 200 million raw nerve fibers screaming between your ears.

In addition to left and right brain activity, memory consists of three types: working memory, short-term memory, and long-term memory.

Working Memory: Your Computer Screen

Working memory is your immediate awareness, which fluctuates continually from one subject to another. "Working memory resides in the frontal lobe and lasts less than a minute. This form of memory is commonly referred to as one's attention span and lasts up to one minute before being erased."[25] Here the mind makes decisions, determines goals, interprets events, and acquires new beliefs, ideas, and opinions. The working memory perceives incoming information, interprets this information by comparing it with past data, and decides whether or not to act based on the incoming and stored information.

Highly sophisticated equipment is now being used to peer into the brain and analyze its various functions and feelings. Colorized brain maps show different colors for different brain activities. Smell an onion; the brain lights up with a color. Pick up a dirty, smelly shirt, and the color changes. View a sunset or kiss your sweetheart, and the colors change again.

Mind-imaging was perfected long before the brain scanners of today. To the dismay of the Pharisees, Jesus, *knowing their thoughts* (Matt. 9:4), x-rayed their thought lives and photographed hidden brain activity. David recognized that God knew his thoughts from afar (Ps. 139:2). What if a mental scanner was developed that showed the thoughts of the person you were talking with? In turn, they could read your thoughts. Yikes! Mental hygiene would suddenly be the most popular self-help class. Thankfully, only Jesus has supernatural mind-reading ability. He knows your thoughts, even before you think them, and he loves you anyway.

THE EDGE

Short-term Memory: Your Random Access Memory

Throughout a day, we access our short-term memory for quick access to information we need. This is "… the material in the mind recallable by focusing attention upon it."[26]

Short-term memory, as the name implies, resides inside the temporal lobes in an area called the "hippocampus"[27] and lasts a relatively short period of time before being erased. In some ways, short-term memory functions as a computer's random access memory. Here you store phone numbers, the names of friends, your bank PIN number, and where you put your keys last night. Whoops! Can't find your keys? Here's why: the mental picture of the location for your keys slipped from the short-term to your long-term memory.

Day One Time Out

Power Thoughts for Your Time Alone with God

Your mind is a powerhouse of potential, one of the most complex objects in the known universe.

- ❑ From your reading, what fact (or facts) about your brain "blows your mind"?

- ❑ Read Psalm 139:13-18 and thank God for your amazing mind. Make it your prayer of thanksgiving today.

- ❑ Why is random chance an inadequate explanation for the complex design of the human mind? Why does the complexity of the human mind argue for a designer with far greater intelligence?

- ❑ Go to the back of your book and cut out or copy this week's meditation verse titled "A Mental Makeover." Carry it with you or put it someplace where you can direct your thoughts to it throughout the day and memorize it.

Long-term Memory: Your Hard-Drive Memory Storage

Often we lament, "I forgot," which is only partially true. It would be more accurate to say, "I remember, but I'm unable to recall." Generally, you don't forget anything; it slips from short-term memory, or as we say, "It just slipped my mind." Our minds contain a huge data bank somewhat like the hard drive of a computer. This is a vast storehouse of experiences, pieces of information, learned behaviors, attitudes, and good as well as bad feelings. By the age of seventy, it's estimated the long-term memory will file 100 trillion pieces of information. To put this into perspective, the *Encyclopedia Britannica* contains approximately 200 million bits of information.[28] This is equivalent to having 500,000 encyclopedia sets stored in your long-term memory. Over a lifetime, the brain erases some things to make room for new memories. Long-term memory is a database that connects our past with our present. When you hear a church bell ringing, the mind will connect with that sound in your memory bank from some time in the past. When you smell cinnamon rolls, it may take you back to the warmth of your mother's kitchen. Or if someone speaks harshly, you'll connect with a moment in the past when someone spoke harshly to you. What's more, the feelings you felt then will surface and shape how you respond now.

Proverbs 12:8 speaks of the danger of a warped mind, and Romans 1:28 speaks of a depraved mind. Like your computer's hard drive, you can input perverse images as well as false data into your long-term memory. The brain's hard drive doesn't sort out what's true or false. As a result, your mind can be programmed with erroneous information, which nonetheless influences your decisions today. This vast data storage of experiences, pieces of information, learned behaviors, and feelings stored in long-term memory, affect behavior in the present.

What about subliminal influence? In 1957, an ad creator, James Vicary, claimed he increased sales of Coca-Cola and popcorn at a movie theater by flashing the words "Eat popcorn" and "Drink Coke" on the screen. The ads flashed by during the movie too quickly to be consciously noticed or spotted with the naked eye. Later, he admitted falsifying the results to gain attention for his business. Subliminal influence remains a debated topic with unproven results.

THE EDGE

How about having an open mind? Yes and no. In *The Living Bible*, Proverbs 8:10 says, *My words are plain and clear to anyone with half a mind—if it is only open! My instruction is far more valuable than silver or gold.* However, many take pride in having an open mind—open to viewing, reading, or listening to anything, without discernment. The result is open minds that need to be closed for repair. Be open to fresh ideas, creative thinking, new ways of doing things, new research, and most of all, to the Word of God. Avoid distorted, perverse thinking, shameful input, gossip, off-color jokes, pornography, and the like—all are powerful in shaping your mind. What you allow to settle in the long-term memory will influence behavior and may come out under certain circumstances. Prior to death, while in an unconscious or delirious state, some begin to talk about information that's been buried in the long-term memory bank. This may be a frightening prospect, but here's the great news: *God can renovate and renew the short-term and long-term memory.* If this weren't possible, attempts at changing behavior would be futile.

I'm thankful for the research and writing of Daniel Amen, M.D., and his help reviewing portions of this chapter.[29] His work includes brain imaging and diagnosis for former NFL players who suffered brain trauma in their careers. Dr. Amen has probably peered into more human brains than anyone in all of history, and he's one of the physicians who worked with Saddleback Church (Lake Forest, California) in the development of *The Daniel Plan*, a food and fitness biblical study.

The drawing that follows illustrates these three types of memory.

WORKING MEMORY
Computer Screen
Immediate awareness usually lasting less than a minute. Input for new information, ideas, interpreting events, and determining actions.

SHORT-TERM MEMORY
Random Access Memory
Material in the mind recallable by focusing attention on it.

LONG-TERM MEMORY
Hard Drive Memory
A vast storehouse of experiences, mental images, pieces of information, learned behaviors, and good as well as bad emotions. By the age of 70, it is estimated the long-term memory will file 100 trillion pieces of information equivalent to 500,000 encyclopedia sets.

Three Types of Memory

© 2015, Dave Beckwith

The Power to Change My Mind

With an understanding of the amazing capacity of the mind and its power to affect our behavior, it makes sense to allow God to control our mind. Here are five steps to get started.

1. **Allow God's Word to scan your mind.**

   For the word of God is living and active. Sharper than any double-edged sword, it penetrates even to dividing soul and spirit, joints and marrow; it judges the thoughts and attitudes of the heart. Nothing in all creation is hidden from God's sight. Everything is uncovered and laid bare before the eyes of him to whom we must give account. (Heb. 4:12-13)

THE EDGE

The Word of God is compared to the sharp, two-edged sword, the *machaira*, used by soldiers in close combat. The double edges and sharp point changed the battle from the "cut and slash" of unwieldy, single-edged swords, six to eight feet in length, to the "stab and thrust" maneuver of a sword about two or three feet in length. Like the machaira, the Word of God delicately cuts and pierces deeper and deeper into your mind, penetrating through your outer facade and revealing what lies deep inside, even to thoughts you're unaware of. Everything is laid bare which may include thoughts like these:

- Resentful feelings
- Buried jealousies and anger
- Empty philosophies
- Anti-God thinking and attitudes
- Hidden fantasies and fetishes
- Obsessions and compulsions
- Regrets
- Hatred, murderous thoughts
- Selfish motives
- Arrogance and cynicism
- Suicidal thoughts
- Pornography
- Sexually perverted images
- Fears and paranoia

All of these are examined with the powerful scalpel of God's Word in the Great Physician's skillful hand.

Buried in your mind is a vast storehouse of information, experiences, and impressions. What's stored in your inner being—the human heart and soul with the will, emotions, and thoughts—is who you are. No person—not your spouse, not your best friend, not even you—knows all your thoughts. But God does. His scan sees all.

> *O LORD, you have searched me and you know me. You know when I sit and when I rise; you perceive my thoughts from afar. You discern my going out and my lying down;*

you are familiar with all my ways. Before a word is on my tongue you know it completely, O LORD. You hem me in—behind and before; you have laid your hand upon me. Such knowledge is too wonderful for me, too lofty for me to attain. (Ps. 139:1-6)

What shows up on God's scan of your mind? Some of the thoughts may be cancer-like images that need surgery for your mental health and well-being.

Hope for Mental Impairment

Most people know of someone suffering some form of mental impairment or reduced mental capacity. Caregivers often wonder, "How much do they understand? Are they capable of understanding spiritual truth?"

I knew Leona Gonzales for about twenty years as her pastor. She shared this remarkable story regarding her husband, Al.

"Al was in the advanced stages of Alzheimer's. He would put his shirt and pants on over his pajamas, shave with a dry razor, and brush his teeth with VO5. He was unable to find different rooms in the house he built when we were married. He recognized me but did not recognize his own daughter or anyone else. Al had always loved working in the yard, but now he spent most of the day on the couch flipping through the *TV Guide*. I continued to pray that he would come to Christ before his earthly life was over.

"One day, while Al and I were watching Nicky Cruz as he preached on the streets of New York, Nicky requested those listening to take the hand of the one next to us. Suddenly, Al was unusually alert, with an amazing mental clarity I had not seen for six years. We were seated at opposite ends of the couch, but he stretched his hand out to grasp mine. He was so intent on the message—his eyes glued to the TV set, and you could see he was lucid and really listening!

"At the end of the message, Nicky Cruz asked us to repeat the sinner's prayer after him. Al did so ALOUD, hearing and repeating every phrase of the prayer! I was thrilled as I watched him. I asked him if he had prayed, and he said, "Yes, did you?" I said I had done it a long time ago. He said, "It wouldn't hurt for you to do it again." Even though Al's mind was ravaged with Alzheimer's, God granted a

> brief window of mental clarity as he understood the gospel, believed in his heart, and confessed faith in Christ with his mouth. Al became a new creation in Christ—new life despite a ravaging disease."
>
> If you have a loved one suffering mental impairment, continue to pray that the Holy Spirit will speak to him or her. Tell that loved one often of God's love, read the Scriptures and play or sing hymns or praise songs with him or her. Often the mind, even with severe disease and loss of mental function, is capable of grasping more than we realize. The Word of God is powerful, penetrating to the division of soul and spirit.

2. Surrender mental strongholds.

The mind is a battleground. For example, you may be in the middle of a worship service at church, and an ugly resentment surfaces in your mind. Everyone is praising God, but you're consumed with seething bitterness and anger. Where did this come from? How do you deal with this mental stronghold?

> *The weapons we fight with are not the weapons of the world. On the contrary, they have divine power to demolish strongholds. We demolish arguments and every pretension that sets itself up against the knowledge of God, and we take captive every thought to make it obedient to Christ. (2 Cor. 10:4-5)*

The mental strongholds are fortresses, the "hide-outs" of destructive thoughts encountered during warfare with godless thinking. Contextually, Paul is talking about those who use speculations and lofty, arrogant words to attack the truth. The phrase *we take captive every thought to make it obedient to Christ* applies this warfare to the full realm of thought life—godless attacks on the truth from things you read and hear and from the fierce battle within your own mind. Camouflaged in secret strongholds, the negative thoughts—fiery darts of the enemy —are capable of vast destruction. From the fortresses in your mind, alarming thoughts may emerge—a seething bitterness, a lustful image, a painful put-down, a subtle jealousy, or a negative feeling.

You may wonder to yourself, *Why do I get these thoughts? If only*

I could stop thinking about ... If someone says, "Do *not* think about yellow monkeys," what happens? Trying *not* to think about yellow monkeys makes it nearly impossible to stop thinking about yellow monkeys. Trying to suppress a thought simply doesn't work. What's the solution? Direct your thoughts to something else. The more you attempt to dismiss a negative, controlling thought, the stronger its grip. Turn your thoughts to a verse of Scripture or other positive thoughts.

Rather than trying to conquer mental strongholds in your own strength, *take captive every thought to make it obedient to Christ* (2 Cor. 10:5). This is spiritual warfare. Imagine Jesus attacking a secret stronghold in the hills of your mind and doing combat with a sinister sniper. Following the battle, he chains the slimy thought and takes it captive. If the thought rears its ugly head again, claim the victory with a prayer: "Lord Jesus, this lust or resentment in my mind is tripping me up. I submit it to you. Take it captive, and by the power of your Word, render it ineffective in my short-term as well as my long-term memory. Amen."

Day Two Time Out

Power Thoughts for Your Time Alone with God

God's power can renovate and renew the short-term and long-term memory.

❑ Return in your reading to Psalm 139. Today read verses 1-6 and 23-24. Make verse 23 your prayer today: *Search me, O God, and know my heart; test me and know my anxious thoughts.*

❑ Ask God to point out to you what he sees on his scan of your mind: resentment, fear, jealousy, cynicism. Make some notes of mental areas to surrender as you allow him to take every thought captive.

3. Renew your mind.

With the surrender of your mental strongholds, you're ready for the transformation of your thought life giving you an edge over Satan's attacks.

> *Therefore, I urge you, brothers, in view of God's mercy, to offer your bodies as living sacrifices, holy and pleasing to God—this is your spiritual act of worship. Do not conform any longer to the pattern of this world, but be transformed by the renewing of your mind. Then you will be able to test and approve what God's will is—his good, pleasing and perfect will.* (Rom. 12:1-2)

At the start of this chapter, I set forth a simple principle: *since the mind controls your behavior, let God control your mind, and your behavior will change.* This is the simple truth of Romans 12:1-2. Verse one says: ... *offer your bodies* [a once-for-all verb tense] *as living sacrifices, holy and pleasing to God.* Verse two is essential to apply verse one: ... *be transformed by the renewing* [a passive present tense verb, meaning a daily process] *of your mind.* God does the renewing as you change the input. My friend Pastor Lou Damiani compared *offering your bodies* to a married couple offering themselves to each other on their wedding day, while the *renewing of the mind* is like the daily rekindling of the love relationship in married life.

The mind controls the body. Renewal transforms the mind. So in practical terms, what does it mean to renew your mind? The word "renew" means to "renovate, refurbish, restore, to make fresh and new." During my college years, I worked part-time as a painter, refurbishing houses that, in some cases, had been repossessed by the bank. Prior to being evicted, some owners destroyed everything possible, beating holes in doors, pulling towel bars out of the walls, destroying the carpet, ripping appliances out and taking them with them. They were angry and bent on destruction. It took a lot of work to transform a beat-up house to look like a new one.

While Satan had control of your thought life, he filled your mind with destructive thoughts, sick attitudes, and stinking thinking. Now he's getting booted out. Before being evicted, he attempts to do as much destruction as possible. Since you've asked Jesus to take control and you're under new ownership, it's time to refurbish and renovate from the inside out.

Regardless of the perverse thoughts that have been stored or the bad attitudes that have gripped you, your mind can be changed. Here's the key: *Do not conform any longer to the pattern of this world* [pressed into compliance or shaped by the world's twisted thinking], *but be transformed* [the Greek word is *metamorpho*] *by the renewing of your mind ...* (Rom. 12:2). Don't feed your mind the world's junk, but be mentally transformed. The word metamorpho is not simply rearranging the furniture in your mind, tidying things up a little. It is a complete renovation, a radical and miraculous change. Not only *what* you think, but the *way* you think is changed. You develop a biblical worldview, a biblical value system that shapes your thoughts and behavior 24/7. The word metamorpho is used only three times in the New Testament: Romans 12:2 and the following two passages. Notice the transformation indicated.

> *Six days later Jesus took Peter, James, and John, and led them up a high mountain to be alone. As the men watched, Jesus' appearance was transformed* (metamorpho, transfigured) *and his clothes became dazzling white, far whiter than any earthly bleach could ever make them.* (Mark 9:2-3 NLT)

> *And we, who with unveiled faces all reflect the Lord's glory, are being transformed* (metamorpho, radically changed) *into his likeness with ever-increasing glory, which comes from the Lord, who is the Spirit.* (2 Cor. 3:18)

Metamorphosis is the change of a worm-like caterpillar into one of God's most beautiful creatures, the butterfly. The 15,000 to 20,000 species of butterflies pass through what scientists consider to be a complete metamorphosis or four distinct stages: from an egg to the larva, then to a caterpillar, and finally, a butterfly. The crawling caterpillar is often a destroyer of plants and crops much like the out-of-control thoughts in your mind that produce destructive behavior. The change into a butterfly brings freedom, beauty, and wonder. Metamorphosis is the word God chose to describe the remarkable change he will perform in your mind.

The Butterfly and Your Psyche

"The ancient Greeks believed that the soul left the body after death in the form of a butterfly. Their symbol for the soul was a butterfly-winged girl named Psyche."[30]

While this is mythology, it is interesting that the Greek word for "soul" in the New Testament is the word *psuche* or "psyche," from3 which the word "psychology" is derived. In addition, Romans 12:2 uses the word that describes the change of a caterpillar into a butterfly (metamorphosis) for God's transformation of the mind. Your "soul" or "psyche" (your mind, will, and emotions) is being transformed from a caterpillar-like state into butterfly-like beauty by metamorphosis.

By the way, did you know the Bible is the greatest book in the world on psychology? It is a "soul book," with hundreds of references to the human soul. The Bible is filled with the greatest insights in the world regarding the human psyche or soul.

Renewing the mind involves changing the input and the content being viewed on the screen of your neck-top computer. Renewing is in the present tense (as previously noted), and this indicates a daily, ongoing process. When you became a believer, you were given the *mind of Christ* (1 Cor. 2:16). This doesn't mean every thought you have as a Christian will be a Christ-like thought, nor does it mean you have a perfect perception of his will for every decision. There'd be no need for our minds to be renewed if we already had the totality of the mind of Christ. Properly understood, the mind of Christ is the enlightenment of Christ through the Holy Spirit to comprehend spiritual truth the natural mind cannot perceive.

Should a believer seek counseling or take medication as prescribed by a doctor? Yes. What is going on in the mind is spiritual, but it is also physical and mental. Biological chemicals—serotonin, dopamine, hormonal levels, etc.—are involved in the healthy function of the mind.

When these chemicals are out of balance, the mind and emotions are greatly affected.

Take depression as an example. If you're living with unconfessed sin, you'll likely be depressed (Psalm 32). However, being depressed doesn't necessarily mean you have unconfessed sin in your life. Depression may be caused by the loss of a loved one, a disappointing setback, buried anger, or a variety of other factors. Counseling will help process these feelings. Depression may also be biological—thyroid dysfunction, illness or disease, chemical imbalance, and a wide variety of other causes. The body, the soul (the thoughts of the mind, will, and emotions), and the spirit are interrelated, with each impacting the other. Being such close neighbors, when one catches something, it affects the others. Effective diagnosis and treatment are always holistic, examining the physical, mental, emotional, and spiritual.

Day Three Time Out

Power Thoughts for Your Time Alone with God

The process of bringing information from the short-term memory to the screen of your mind and reflecting on it is called meditation—the key to renewing your mind.

❑ Read Romans 12:1-2 in your Bible and then compare it to this paraphrase.

So here's what I want you to do, God helping you: Take your everyday, ordinary life—your sleeping, eating, going-to-work, and walking-around life—and place it before God as an offering. Embracing what God does for you is the best thing you can do for him. Don't become so well-adjusted to your culture that you fit into it without even thinking. Instead, fix your attention on God. You'll be changed from the inside out. Readily recognize what he wants from you, and quickly respond to it. Unlike the culture around you, always dragging you down to its level of immaturity, God brings the best out of you, develops well-formed maturity in you. (Rom. 12:1-2 MSG)

❑ Sit at your kitchen table and place a mug on the table in front of you and one across from you. Enjoy a beverage and treat if you'd like. Now settle in to have a conversation with Jesus. I encourage you to talk out loud if you feel the freedom to do so. Read Romans 12:1-2, slowly and thoughtfully reflecting on each phrase. During your conversation with Jesus, discuss these thoughts with him.

- *When did you first offer or present your body to him?*
- *What joy did this bring to you?*
- *What have been the struggles to stay committed?*
- *Tell him about the pressures around you to conform to the thoughts of the world.*
- *What is his plan for you to renew your mind?*
- *Ask him to help you respond to his nudging.*
- *Visualize the impact on your life when your mind is transformed.*
- *Thank him for what he will do.*

4. Develop a plan for daily meditation.

I'm skeptical when someone tells of some secret formula that guarantees success. But when God says, "Do this, and you will be successful," I'm tuned in. Many people think prosperity and success come from having power and money, a winning attitude, influential personal contacts, working long hours, and a relentless desire to get ahead. Instead, God promises success for the person who develops and cultivates a simple practice: meditation. This is the success-edge to win in this high-pressure, intimidating world.

> *Be strong and courageous, for you are the one who will lead these people to possess all the land I swore to their ancestors I would give them. Be strong and very courageous. Be careful to obey all the instructions Moses gave you. Do not deviate from them, turning either to the right or to the left. Then you will be successful in everything you do. Study this Book of Instruction continually. Meditate on it day and night so you will be sure to obey everything written in it. Only then will you prosper and succeed in all you do. This is my command—be strong and courageous! Do not be afraid or discouraged. For the LORD your God is with you wherever you go.* (Josh. 1:6-9 NLT)

My hunch is that Joshua was shaking in his sandals as he stepped into the leadership role vacated by the great leader Moses. How do you follow a leader whom God used to humble the most powerful nation of the day by calling down supernatural plagues, a leader who carried a big stick that split the Red Sea, a leader who came down from a mountain with the Ten Commandments directly from God, a leader who struck a rock and water poured forth, and a leader who spoke directly with God on a regular basis? Joshua also faced the daunting task of conquering thirty-one kings in the battles for the Promised Land.

Joshua had every reason to be intimidated. God knew this, so he gave Joshua the resource to overcome intimidation. Look at Joshua 1:6-9, and underline the three times the phrase *be strong and very courageous*

THE EDGE

appears. Feeling inadequate and intimidated are common weaknesses. What changes inadequacy into strength and intimidation into courage? *Biblical meditation is intimidation medication.*

What is meditation? Many think of meditation as something monks do isolated from people while sitting on a hillside eating bird seed. Others associate meditation with various forms of eastern mysticism—emptying the mind while sitting cross-legged on a rug in a semi-trance. This is *not* biblical meditation. An empty mind is a vulnerable mind. Never does the Bible tell us to empty our minds. J. I. Packer, writing in his classic work *Knowing God*, says,

Meditation is the activity of calling to mind, and thinking over, and dwelling on, and applying to oneself, the various things that one knows about the works and ways and purposes and promises of God. It is an activity of holy thought, consciously performed in the presence of God, under the eye of God, by the help of God, as a means of communion with God.[31]

Below, stated briefly, is my summation of why developing the practice of meditation will have such a great impact on your life.

Biblical Meditation

… isn't emptying your mind; it's filling your mind with God.
… doesn't require isolation; it fits with the flow of your busy life.
… doesn't complicate your life; it's your compass in the midst of chaos.
… overcomes intimidation with God-courage (Josh. 1:6-9).
… builds strong faith (Rom. 10:17).
… will help you overcome temptation (Ps. 119:11).
… is God's prescription to heal your mind and emotions (Rom. 12:1-2).
… is an effective antidote to worry (Phil. 4:6-8).
… changes your attitude and outlook on life (Phil. 4:7).
… brings success to your endeavors (Ps. 1:2-3).
… is the key to perfect peace (Isa. 26:3).

Nicholas Carr, in his book titled *The Shallows: What the Internet Is Doing to Our Brains*, contends that the Internet has brought a drought of deep thinking and ability to concentrate on a subject. He affirms the many benefits of the Internet—banking, real-time news, shopping, research, communication, email—but laments that the more time we spend on the Web, jumping from one site to another, the more incapable we become of concentrating. We lose the ability to think deeply about a subject. Biblical meditation refocuses the working mind over and over again to a singular thought or verse, allowing it to be analyzed, amplified, and applied. It is like holding a sparkling diamond up to the light and seeing it from every angle possible. Biblical meditation is a return to deep thinking about God and eternal issues.

Scripture memorization is a wonderful way to retain God's Word and have it available whenever you need it. The Psalmist wrote, *I have hidden your word in my heart that I might not sin against you* (Ps. 119:11). However, many people have a "mental block" regarding memorizing, and they often protest, "I can't even remember someone's name." I was surprised to discover the words "memorize" and "memorization" are not found in the Bible even though Jewish training included memorizing Scripture, and memorization is implied in Psalm 119:11. Instead, the Bible frequently uses the word "meditate." Personally, I've memorized many verses by repeatedly meditating on them. The by-product of repeated meditation is memorization, and memorization helps facilitate meditation. Focus on daily meditation, and you'll be surprised how easy it is to memorize the verse. Because of God's emphasis on Scripture meditation, I believe this is the key to transforming the mind and changing behavior. Yes, I recommend memorizing Scripture, but use meditation as the process to facilitate memorization.

Closely associated with meditating on God's Word is the word "delight"—a word found nine times in Psalm 119, the great chapter on biblical meditation. The Hebrew word for "delight" means "to sport, to play with, to take delight in." If you're excited about the purchase of a new electronic gadget, you take delight in it by playing with it, fiddling around with it, discovering all of its features. The best way to grasp the "how to" for the electronic gadget is to have fun with it. If you approach it as drudgery, learning it will be much more difficult. Educators affirm that the most effective learning is fun, not a laborious grind. While I'm not suggesting manipulating the meaning of a verse, when you meditate on Scripture, take delight in it, play with it in your mind, think about it in new and interesting ways, analyze it, amplify it, apply it, pray about it, sing about it, rejoice in it, and even dance to it. David said *I dance to the tune of your revelation* (Ps. 119:70 MSG), an appropriate paraphrase of *I delight in your law*. Enjoying the music of meditating will strengthen you as you walk through tough times: *If your revelation hadn't delighted me so, I would have given up when the hard times came* (Ps. 119:92 MSG). While meditation doesn't require isolation, it's helpful to have moments when you get alone for fifteen to twenty minutes or more to meditate.

Daily meditating on the thoughts of God makes it easy to "talk it through" with the family in teachable moments during the day.

> *These commandments that I give you today are to be upon your hearts. Impress them on your children. Talk about them when you sit at home and when you walk along the road, when you lie down and when you get up. Tie them as symbols on your hands and bind them on your foreheads. Write them on the doorframes of your houses and on your gates.* (Deut. 6:6-9)

More than reading a verse in the morning, allow God's Word to saturate your thoughts throughout the day. Learn to think biblically. Put verses on the refrigerator, the bathroom mirror, your computer screen, or your desk at work. Tuck verse cards with the napkin holder so you can talk about them during the evening meal. Bible software is available for your computer as well as other electronic devices. I have nine versions of the Bible on my cell phone, and I'll often flip it open to read a few verses while I'm waiting in line. As a teenager, I memorized all the verses in the *Topical Memory System* developed by the Navigators. I still carry these verses with me, and I direct my thoughts to them when I have a few spare minutes. AWANA is a wonderful program to get your children started memorizing and valuing Scripture. The Bible is also available on CDs or DVDs. Use your commute time to listen to CDs or tune in your radio to some excellent Christian teaching. It will transform your mind and change your life!

Never have there been more resources to enable biblical meditation—and never have there been more distractions to interfere with practicing biblical meditation. Make it a top priority.

Day Four Time Out

Power Thoughts for Your Time Alone with God

Biblical meditation refocuses the working mind over and over again to a singular thought or verse, allowing it to be analyzed, amplified, and applied. It is like holding a sparkling diamond up to the light and seeing it from every angle possible.

- ❏ To practice meditation, ask God to speak to your heart, and then read a passage of Scripture (use more than one translation if available). After reading it, go back and take it phrase by phrase, mentally "chewing on" on each key thought. What does this mean in practical terms? How do I apply this to my life? Then pray the thoughts of the passage back to God using your own words. You may choose to stay in one passage for a day or even a week. Allow the passage to become part of who you are.

- ❏ Now let's practice biblical meditation. Read Psalm 1:1-3 and Deuteronomy 6:6-9 in your Bible, and then compare it to the paraphrases below.

Oh, the joys of those who do not follow evil men's advice, who do not hang around with sinners, scoffing at the things of God. But they delight in doing everything God wants them to, and day and night are always meditating on his laws and thinking about ways to follow him more closely. They are like trees along a riverbank bearing luscious fruit each season without fail. Their leaves shall never wither, and all they do shall prosper. (Ps. 1:1-3 TLB)

And you must think constantly about these commandments I am giving you today. You must teach them to your children and talk about them when you are at home or out for a walk; at bedtime and the first thing in the morning. Tie them on your finger, wear them on your forehead, and write them on the doorposts of your house. (Deut. 6:6-9 TLB)

5. Guard your mind.

Be careful what you think, because your thoughts run your life (Prov. 4:23 NCV). What a sobering thought. Your life can run amuck or succeed depending on what goes on between your ears. The computer world uses the phrase, "Beware of GIGO." This means "garbage in, garbage out," and this is true for your God-designed neck-top computer as well.

Solomon, in a man-to-man talk with his sons, warned, *Above all else, guard your affections. For they influence everything else in your life: ... Look straight ahead; don't even turn your head to look* (Prov. 4:23, 25 TLB). He was talking about a sensual woman. The visual cortex is more active in men than in women. As a result, pornographic images get a stronger grip on the mind of a man. Most men find it difficult to look away from a pornographic image because their mental receiver locks into the strong visual signal. William Struthers in *Wired for Intimacy: How Pornography Hijacks the Male Brain* says, "As men fall deeper into the mental habit of fixating on sexual images, the exposure to them creates neural pathways. With each lingering stare, pornography deepens a Grand Canyon-like gorge in the brain through which images of women are destined to flow."[32] Chemicals released in the neural pathways of the brain lead to a rewiring that is similar to drug addiction, causing the viewer to need more. Clay Olsen, executive director of Fight the New Drug, says, "Studies have shown that individuals who regularly consume pornography can end up preferring the computer screen to a human being to get their sexual fix."[33] What goes on in the mind will affect behavior sooner or later. Conversely, when behavior is acted out, it creates a neural pathway in the brain, which in turn reinforces the behavior. Paul warned about the grip of sexual sin and confirmed that sinning without restraint yields a depraved mind (Rom. 1:24-32).

> *He* [God] *gave them over to a depraved mind, to do what ought not to be done. They have become filled with every kind of wickedness, evil, greed and depravity. They are full of envy, murder, strife, deceit, and malice. They are gossips, slanderers, God-haters, insolent, arrogant and boastful; they invent ways of doing evil; they disobey*

THE EDGE

their parents; they are senseless, faithless, heartless, ruthless. (Rom. 1:28-31)

The good news is that healthy mental patterns and sexual appetites can be reestablished by intentionally redirecting the neurochemical flow and renewing the mind in the Word of God. Thought patterns and behavior are inseparable. For this reason, guard your mind as if it were Ft. Knox, the heavily fortified U.S. Mint depository for bullion deposits and gold reserves.

However, I don't recommend isolating from the world or cutting off all awareness of current events. To maintain a perspective on world events, I read several magazines, including *TIME, WORLD, Christianity Today, Decision,* and several others. My friend and long-time mentor, Dr. George Cowan, President Emeritus of Wycliffe Bible Translators, along with his wife, Florie, combined prayer with watching the evening news. Together they'd view a report of developments in some part of the world. When the commercial came on, they hit the mute button and prayed for that area of the world. They knew missionaries in nearly every part of the world, so they prayed specifically for them by name.

How do you choose content that is acceptable in a movie, book, or television show? First, check the Internet to review the content and ratings in advance. Next, be sensitive to how it may affect others, especially children. My wife reacts differently than I do to watching an intense, suspenseful program. I've learned to check with her before assuming she wants to see a particular program. We stop a movie after only a few minutes if we feel the content is inappropriate or if the movie looks like a senseless waste of time.

It is a fact that the Bible has some violent scenes (check out the book of Judges), and sexuality is presented in appropriate detail in several places. Some parts of the Bible would likely be rated at least PG-13. But why is the content in the Bible, even when it describes immoral or violent scenes, different from much of today's media content? With biblical content, God is God, sin is sin, right and wrong have consequences, truth is not relative, and morality is clear. In today's media, blurred morality is a dangerous and subtle form of indoctrination. Sex outside of marriage is taken for granted: "Hey, everybody's doing it, so what's wrong with you?" Profanity and cursing are commonplace. Right and wrong are mocked, while tolerance of sin is applauded. Cheating is okay if you can get away with it. Anti-God thinking is subtly introduced and woven into the tapestry of a media-distorted worldview.

Has it always been this way? On December 6, 1951, the National Association of Broadcasters enacted a Television Code that governed the content of TV. It blended the codes of the three networks—ABC, CBS, and NBC—in an attempt to prevent government regulation. Nearly all US television programs from 1952 through the early 1980s complied with the code, and this was indicated by the "Seal of Good Practice" in the closing credits. What was in the code?

> The code prohibited the use of profanity, the negative portrayal of family life, irreverence for God and religion, illicit sex, drunkenness and addiction, presentation of cruelty, detailed techniques of crime, the use of horror for its own sake, and the negative portrayal of law enforcement officials, among others. The code regulated how performers should dress and move to be within the "bounds of decency." Further, news reporting was to be "factual, fair and without bias" and commentary and analysis should be "clearly defined as such."[34]

It was revised several times before being suspended in 1983 due to a settlement with the Justice Department. Here are some of the moral and ethical standards from the "Code of Practices for Television Broadcasters," with the section and paragraph indicated (the headings are supplied).

> **Language:** (a) Profanity, obscenity, smut and vulgarity are forbidden, even when likely to be understood only by part of the audience.
>
> **Faith:** (b) Attacks on religion and religious faiths are not allowed. Reverence is to mark any mention of God, his attributes and powers.
>
> **Marriage and divorce:** (d) Respect is maintained for the sanctity of marriage and the value of the home.

THE EDGE

Divorce is not treated casually nor justified as a solution for marital problems."

Sex and nudity: (e) Illicit sex relations are not treated as commendable. (f) Sex crimes and abnormalities are generally unacceptable as program material. From the section on "Decency and Decorum in Production": (1) The costuming of all performers shall be within the bounds of propriety and shall avoid such exposure or such emphasis on anatomical detail as would embarrass or offend home viewers.

Substance abuse: (g) Drunkenness and narcotic addiction are never presented as desirable or prevalent.

Occult: (l) Exhibitions of fortune-telling, astrology ... palm-reading, and numerology are acceptable only when required by a plot of the theme of a program, and then the presentation should be developed in a manner designed not to foster superstition or excite interest of belief in these subjects.

Crime: (q) Criminality shall be presented as undesirable and unsympathetic. The condoning of crime and the treatment of the commission of crime in a frivolous, cynical or callous manner is unacceptable.

Horror: (s) The use of horror for its own sake will be eliminated; the use of visual or aural effects which would shock or alarm the viewer, and the detailed presentation of brutality or physical agony by sight or by sound are not permissible.

A lot has changed; the standards of decency have nose-dived. Little by little, we've grown accustomed to what we considered unacceptable a few decades ago. "The regulations for content laid down by the Television

Code almost sound quaint by modern standards, but they provide a startling glimpse into how much our culture has changed in the past 50 years."[35] No one would dare call it brainwashing (after all, we do have a choice in what we view), but we've grown quite comfortable being conformed to the world rather than being transformed by renewing our minds with the thoughts of God (Rom. 12:2).

Allow the Holy Spirit to guide you in the development of your personal standards to guard your mind. "Changing Channels on My Mind," which follows, is a grid to check the content of movies or television. Be courageous and willing for the Holy Spirit to check what you feed your mind.

Changing Channels on My Mind

Fix your thoughts on what is true, and honorable, and right, and pure, and lovely, and admirable. Think about things that are excellent and worthy of praise. (Phil. 4:8 NLT)

✓ Check your television and movie choices with this worksheet and discuss it with the family.

Positive Values
✓ Does the TV program or movie uphold values such as these?

- ❏ Kindness (compassion, tenderness, gentleness, value for people)
- ❏ Family Values (morally uplifting, clear standards of right and wrong)
- ❏ Humor (clean jokes and situational comedy)
- ❏ Respect (authority is honored: God, government, police, schools, parents, and employers)
- ❏ Excellence (uplifting, valuable, worthwhile)
- ❏ Truth (accurate portrayal of right and wrong, informative, provides a window to learn and better understand the world, does not distort God's truth)
- ❏ Faith (God is recognized as the giver and sustainer of life; religious life and personal belief are respected)
- ❏ Other: _____

Negative Values
✓ Does the TV program or movie glorify these behaviors?
Are they practiced without consequences, applauded as normal, or presented in enticing ways?

- ❏ Immorality (sexually suggestive language or scenes, sex outside of marriage, etc.)
- ❏ Profanity (swearing, foul or abusive language)
- ❏ Violence (destruction of life and property, murder, abuse, rape, etc.)
- ❏ Rebellion (disobedience to parents, defiance of God)
- ❏ Occult (astrology, witchcraft, sorcery, horoscopes)
- ❏ Greed (materialism, drugs, greed)
- ❏ Racism (hatred based on ethnic origin)
- ❏ Other: _____

Be clear about your own choices, but guard against being legalistic in imposing your standards on others. Allow the Holy Spirit to direct your life as well as theirs. In other words, don't play Holy Spirit in another person's life. Whether you're watching TV, talking with a friend, choosing a movie, or surfing the Web, ask yourself this: *Are my thoughts pleasing to God? Is Jesus comfortable viewing the screen of my mind with me?* Join the Psalmist David in praying, *May the words of my mouth and the meditation of my heart be pleasing in your sight, O Lord, my Rock and my Redeemer* (Ps. 19:14).

Transformation of Your Mind: What to Expect

When you cooperate with God in consistently renewing your mind over a period of time, God promises metamorphosis, worm-to-butterfly transformation. But what is happening in your long-term memory, your mental hard drive? Do memories of rejection, jealousy, or lustful thoughts disappear? Does the memory of a tragic accident vanish? Do you forget being abused as a child? I acknowledge that I don't fully understand the process, but I testify that God is transforming my mind—healing the scars of rejection, abuse, perverse images, and a distorted view of myself. Here are four aspects of what to expect when God transforms your mind.

1. Mental metamorphosis changes the content of your mind.

This is rock-solid biblical truth. The Word of God penetrates like a two-edged sword into the depths of your inner thought life, exposing the mental images, memories, and attitudes of the heart (Heb. 4:12-13). God works within your mind to demolish mental strongholds as you take every thought captive in obedience to Christ (2 Cor. 10:3-5). This reminds us that the mind will always be a battleground. Temptations come via our thoughts, which must be continually surrendered to Christ. As you renew your mind, God transforms it by the power of his Word (Rom. 12:2).

2. Mental metamorphosis also changes the way your mind thinks.

Deep inside your mind, you have a set of thinking that shapes the way you look at everything. This is your worldview, and it shapes all of your reality. With the transformation of your mind, your worldview is radically changed to a biblical worldview. How you look at family life, social justice, business ethics, entertainment, environmental issues, death and life, moral behavior, right and wrong, and virtually every area of life is shaped by your biblical worldview. Seeing things as God sees them means absolute moral truths exist as defined by Scripture. Your mind now processes information through the lens of biblical truth.

3. Mental metamorphosis allows the Holy Spirit to give you spiritual insight.

The natural mind is incapable of understanding the things of God. *The man without the Spirit does not accept the things that come from the Spirit of God, for they are foolishness to him, and he cannot understand them* (1 Cor. 2:14 NIV). But with the flashlight of the Holy Spirit illuminating our minds, we are given insights into what God has prepared for us.

> *"No eye has seen, no ear has heard, and no mind has imagined what God has prepared for those who love him." But it was to us that God revealed these things by his Spirit. For his Spirit searches out everything and shows us God's deep secrets.* (1 Cor. 2:9-10 NLT)

We sometimes think the *No eye ... no ear ... no mind has imagined* is what we'll understand when we're in heaven. But notice these things have been revealed *now* by the Holy Spirit. We have been given the mind of Christ—unique insight and understanding of spiritual things revealed by the Holy Spirit (1 Cor. 2:16).

4. Mental metamorphosis diffuses and selectively overwrites buried mental images.

In practical terms, what happens to buried anger, jealousies, woundedness, and pornography stored in your long-term memory? You may suffer from deeply scarring memories or traumatic events that it seems you will always remember. A thought can be like a land mine, a buried device that explodes when you walk or drive over it. Someone may get too close to a buried wound and suddenly you have an emotional explosion. As military land mines can be diffused through a "render safe procedure" (RSP), mental land mines can also be diffused. For example, I can remember many of the events when I've been hurt, but I no longer feel resentment. The Word of God has diffused the memory. It is no longer explosive, and I am set free from its influence.

In the computer world, the only way to permanently erase a file is to overwrite it repeatedly. Hitting DELETE or FORMAT does not permanently remove files—only the visible pathways to the files. Computer files are permanently erased by a process called "disk wiping" or disk scrubbing"—actually overwriting the unwanted files with new data several times. The government standard (DoD 5220.22-M), considered a medium security level, specifies overwriting a hard drive six times with repetitive numbers.[36]

We've become familiar with terms like malware, viruses, spyware, Trojan horses, and worms that work havoc in our computers. I believe God selectively overwrites the corrupted files in our minds—fears and phobias, scarring put-downs, pornographic images, buried resentments—with forgiveness, joy, patience, courage, gentleness, peace, tenderness, and love. This is the repetitive power of renewing the mind (Rom. 12:2), continually meditating on Scripture as it overwrites the old destructive data.

For example, if your mother screamed at you, "You're a worthless, no good child. You'll never amount to anything," this lie is burned into your mental hard drive. The brain's hard drive doesn't sort out what's true or false. It will be very difficult *not* to act like a worthless, no good person. As a Christian, you begin to read your Bible. This becomes "your place of quiet retreat" as you wait for the Word to renew you (Ps. 119:114 MSG). And one day you read these amazing verses.

> *Even before he made the world, God loved us and chose us in Christ to be holy and without fault in his eyes. God decided in advance to adopt us into his own family by bringing us to himself through Jesus Christ. This is what he wanted to do, and it gave him great pleasure.* (Eph. 1:4-5 NLT)

THE EDGE

Wow! God chose me and adopted me into his family, you think to yourself. As you continue to read and meditate, the Word of God is repeatedly overwriting that old "you're a worthless, no-good person, who will never amount to anything" file. Your view of yourself changes. You begin to carry yourself differently. You're a child of God adopted into an eternal family. You're the apple of God's eye (Ps. 17:8). As you meditate on Scripture, you are overwriting the damaging lie your mother planted in your mind. You will likely always remember what you're mother told you, but the false data is written over with new transforming information.

Here's another illustration of what takes place. Before you became a Christian, when certain things went wrong, you may have cut loose with a rapid-fire string of profanity. It was like a trigger on a pistol that unleashed a bullet barrage of cursing and swearing. This nearly automatic response was rooted in your memory bank. Once you become a believer, the Holy Spirit convicts you about the filth that comes out of your mouth when you're upset. You begin to meditate on Scriptures that remind you to not let any unwholesome word proceed from your mouth (Eph. 4:29). The Word begins to overwrite the trigger response and the day comes when an event occurs that makes you very angry. In the past, this would have triggered a string of profanity, but now you no longer swear as you once did. This is "metamorphosis of the mind."

The brain-computer comparisons may help us understand our minds in some measure, but in the final analysis, the analogy falls short of grasping the complexity of the human mind. As God's Word penetrates into our minds and mental strongholds are taken captive, buried negative thoughts and feelings are diffused, written over, and selectively erased; the destructive fangs are removed, and their controlling influence is rendered null and void. God's Word overpowers these potentially destructive thoughts. The drawing that follows illustrates the transformation process.

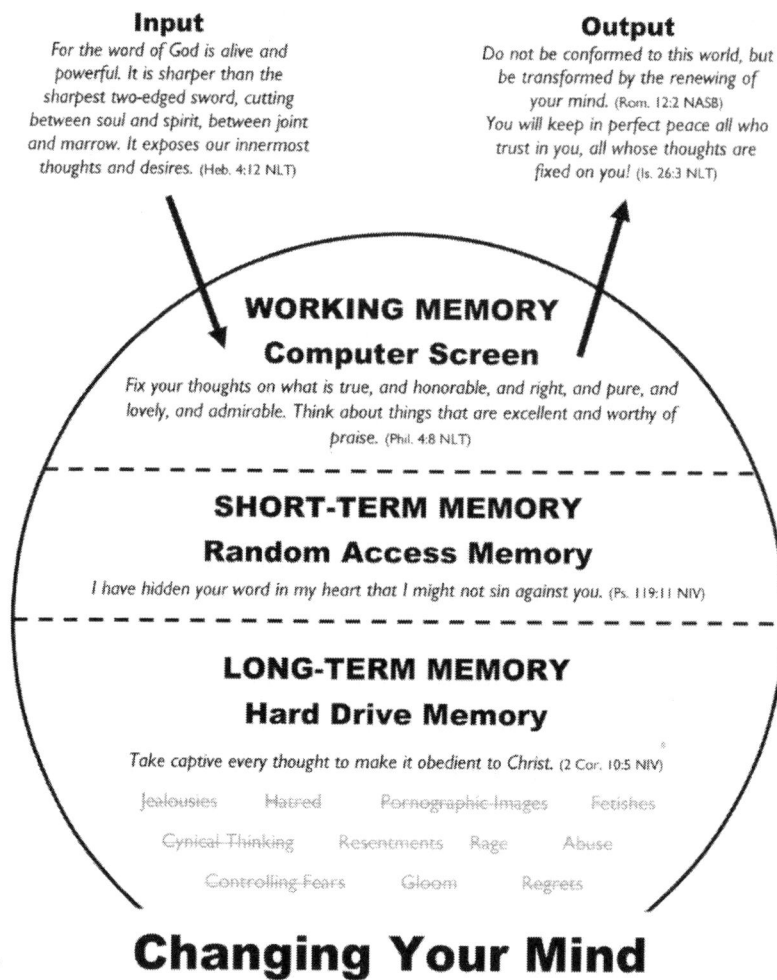

Input
For the word of God is alive and powerful. It is sharper than the sharpest two-edged sword, cutting between soul and spirit, between joint and marrow. It exposes our innermost thoughts and desires. (Heb. 4:12 NLT)

Output
Do not be conformed to this world, but be transformed by the renewing of your mind. (Rom. 12:2 NASB) *You will keep in perfect peace all who trust in you, all whose thoughts are fixed on you!* (Is. 26:3 NLT)

WORKING MEMORY
Computer Screen
Fix your thoughts on what is true, and honorable, and right, and pure, and lovely, and admirable. Think about things that are excellent and worthy of praise. (Phil. 4:8 NLT)

SHORT-TERM MEMORY
Random Access Memory
I have hidden your word in my heart that I might not sin against you. (Ps. 119:11 NIV)

LONG-TERM MEMORY
Hard Drive Memory
Take captive every thought to make it obedient to Christ. (2 Cor. 10:5 NIV)

~~Jealousies~~   ~~Hatred~~   ~~Pornographic Images~~   ~~Fetishes~~
~~Cynical Thinking~~   ~~Resentments~~   ~~Rage~~   ~~Abuse~~
~~Controlling Fears~~   ~~Gloom~~   ~~Regrets~~

Changing Your Mind

© 2015. Dave Beckwith

Go Ahead and Change Your Mind

It's your right to "change your mind." No one can stop you. So what's holding you back? Start reading and meditating on God's Word every day.

Biblical meditation gives you *an edge* to win, to be successful in your endeavors. As David said, *Your commands give me an edge on my enemies; they never become obsolete* (Ps. 119:98 MSG). Your mind is a powerhouse of potential. Unleash God's power to transform your

THE EDGE

neck-top computer that controls your every impulse, behavior, decision, feeling, action, or reaction. And remember, *since your mind controls your behavior, let God control your mind and your behavior will change.*

Or to put it more simply, to quote some unknown poet,

>Your mind is a garden,
>Your thoughts are seeds.
>You can grow flowers, or
>Just grow weeds.

So what's growing in your garden?

Day Five Time Out

Power Thoughts for Your Time Alone with God

The Word of God diffuses buried negative thoughts and feelings rendering them null and void—the destructive fangs are removed.

❏ Read Philippians 4:4-8 in your Bible and then compare it with this paraphrase.

Delight yourselves in God, yes, find your joy in him at all times. Have a reputation for gentleness, and never forget the nearness of your Lord. Don't worry over anything whatever; tell God every detail of your needs in earnest and thankful prayer, and the peace of God which transcends human understanding, will keep constant guard over your hearts and minds as they rest in Christ Jesus. Here is a last piece of advice. If you believe in goodness and if you value the approval of God, fix your minds on the things which are holy and right and pure and beautiful and good. Model your conduct on what you have learned from me, on what I have told you and shown you, and you will find the God of peace will be with you. (Phil. 4:4-8 Phillips NT)

❏ What is your "game plan" to guard your mind? What are your personal standards? Write out your plan. Use a separate sheet of paper if necessary.

STRENGTH TEAM

SESSION THREE
CHANGING MY MIND

Your mind is a powerhouse of potential, one of the most complex objects in the known universe. The component parts are staggering: one hundred billion nerve cells connecting with each other up to 60,000 times through 100,000 miles of nerve fibers—all of this going on between your ears. Wise Solomon said it this way, *Be careful what you think because your thoughts run your life* (Prov. 4:23 NCV). Since your mind controls your behavior, let God control your mind, and your behavior will change. Now is the time to let God take control of your mind. It's your right to "change your mind," so let's do it.

CONNECT

Choose one of the following as your opener:

- ❑ Tell about a time when a smell, taste, sound, or sight triggered a warm memory—or an unpleasant memory.

- ❑ In junior high, high school, or college, what pressure did you feel to fit in and conform to the crowd? How is it different or similar now?

GROW

- ❑ Discuss the drawing of the mind that follows. Pause after each part of the drawing and discuss it. Identify examples of how a violent TV program or an off-color story you hear at work gets stuck in your memory.

THE EDGE

- ❑ Read Philippians 4:4-9 phrase by phrase, pausing to unwrap each key thought.

  Rejoice in the Lord always. I will say it again: Rejoice! Let your gentleness be evident to all. The Lord is near. Do not be anxious about anything, but in everything, by prayer and petition, with thanksgiving, present your requests to God. And the peace of God, which transcends all understanding, will guard your hearts and your minds in Christ Jesus. Finally, brothers, whatever is true, whatever is noble, whatever is right, whatever is pure, whatever is lovely, whatever is admirable—if anything is excellent or praiseworthy—think about such things. (Phil. 4:4-8)

- ❑ For vivid contrast, as a group, select an opposite value to insert in verse 8 to replace each positive value. The first opposite is supplied to show how this works.

- ❑ *Whatever is false* (the opposite of true), *whatever is _____ (noble), whatever is _____ (right), whatever is _____ (pure), whatever is _____ (lovely), whatever is _____ (admirable)—if anything is _____ (excellent) or _____ (praiseworthy)—think about such things.*

  When finished, read it out loud with the negative words inserted. How similar is this to the culture around you?

- ❑ Optional: discuss these questions as time permits.

  • Why do you think God didn't erase the hard drive of our brains to remove destructive thoughts and memories when we accepted Christ?

  • Have you found this to be true? *Your commands give me an edge on my enemies; they never become obsolete* (Psalm 119:98 MSG). In what ways?

- What is your worldview? Is it a biblical worldview?
- Discuss the best way to guide and protect children in choices regarding television, Internet, movies, and video games?

❑ Read aloud in unison the "Changing My Mind" verse for this week.

> **A Mental Makeover**
> *Don't copy the behavior and customs of this world, but let God transform you into a new person by changing the way you think.*
> (Rom. 12:2 NLT)
> **Changing My Mind – Week 3**

APPLY

❑ What are the negative mental influences (TV, movies, reading, work environment, etc.) you face each week?

❑ As a group, read and discuss these benefits of biblical meditation.

Biblical Meditation

… isn't emptying your mind; it's filling your mind with God.

… doesn't require isolation; it fits with the flow of your busy life.

… doesn't complicate your life; it's your compass in the midst of chaos.

… overcomes intimidation with God-courage (Josh. 1:6-9).

… builds strong faith (Rom. 10:17).

Input

"For the word of God is living and active and sharper than any two-edged sword, and piercing as far as the division of soul and spirit, of both joints and marrow, and able to judge the thoughts and intentions of the heart"
(Heb. 4:12 NASB).

Output

"Do not be conformed to this world, but be transformed by the renewing of your mind," (Rom. 12:2 NASB). "You will keep in perfect peace all who trust in you, all whose thoughts are fixed on you!"
(Is. 26:3 NLT).

WORKING MEMORY
Computer Screen

"Fix your thoughts on what is true, and honorable, and right, and pure, and lovely, and admirable. Think about things that are excellent and worthy of praise"
(Phil. 4:8 NLT).

SHORT-TERM MEMORY
Random Access Memory

"I have hidden your word in my heart, that I might not sin against you (Ps. 119:11 NLT).

LONG-TERM MEMORY
Hard Drive Memory

"We are taking every thought captive to the obedience of Christ," (2 Cor. 10:4-5 NASB).

Jealousies Hatred Pornographic Images Fetishes
Cynical Thinking Resentments Rage Abuse
Controlling Fears Gloom Regrets

Changing Your Mind
© 2012. Dave Beckwith

… will help you overcome temptation (Ps. 119:11).

… is God's prescription to heal your mind and emotions (Rom. 12:1-2).

… is an effective antidote to worry (Phil. 4:6-8).

… changes your attitude and outlook on life (Phil. 4:7).

… brings success to your endeavors (Ps. 1:2-3).

… is the key to perfect peace (Isa. 26:3).

☐ What is your "game plan" for practicing meditation? Share it with the group.

PRAY

☐ Spend time praying for each other with brief sentence prayers. Close by praying this prayer out loud in unison.

May the words of my mouth and the meditation of my heart be pleasing in your sight, O LORD, my Rock and my Redeemer. (Ps. 19:14)

SHARE

☐ Look for an opportunity to start a conversation this week. Here are some questions that may start a dialogue:

- *Do you think the human mind can be changed?*
- *What weighs heavily on your mind about our world today?*
- *How do you handle anxiety and stress?*

☐ Let this be your prayer as you ask God to lead you to someone to share your faith with. *Always be prepared to give an answer to everyone who asks you to give the reason for the hope that you have. But do this with gentleness and respect* (1 Pet. 3:15).

EXTRA

If you have additional time, enjoy reading Psalm 119, the longest chapter in the Bible and the classic section on how God's Word will change your life. See Appendix C for a worksheet to use as you go through Psalm 119.

CHAPTER FOUR
RELEASING RESENTMENTS

It takes a strong person to forgive.

We were excited to have guests joining us for lunch at our home for a Good Friday celebration. All the preparations had been made, and the food was on the table. Just before I led in prayer, Joanne took a phone call in the office and motioned for the group to go ahead and eat. About thirty minutes later, she returned to the table with tears running down her cheeks. Her tears created an awkward moment for the guests and us as well. Sensing her pain and embarrassment, I put my arm around her and asked, "Who was that on the phone? What happened?" Through her tears, she attempted to explain that one of the leading women of the church had verbally ripped into her.

Easter Sunday had been planned as a big community outreach, and Joanne, as administrative secretary for the church where I served as pastor, had attempted to shore up an area that seemed to have been overlooked. This woman and her husband felt Joanne's well-intended efforts were meddling in their area. Joanne quickly apologized hoping to put the matter to rest, but for some reason, it remained unresolved. This woman's words hurt deeply, and her unwillingness to accept Joanne's apology hurt even worse.

The Easter services were packed with record attendance and many decisions for Christ, but the joy we felt was clouded by what had happened. Usually, the misunderstanding would have been quickly resolved and forgotten; instead, it festered and escalated into a bitter distrust of our leadership. As the conflict continued to intensify, Joanne drove her car to a quiet spot and sobbed. Crying out to God, she asked, "Why?" It didn't make sense. She'd done nothing with ill will. Her efforts were intended to help a ministry, and now she was being maligned for her hard work.

The couple had been at the church for many years and had a significant power base. They wanted an austere atmosphere in the services, and they felt everyone should enter the sanctuary and sit in silence before the service began. During the service, any outburst of laughter or spontaneous applause was, in their way of thinking, disgraceful. However, we encouraged warm interaction, humor, and spontaneous clapping when appropriate. These differences set in motion an intense struggle, all of it fueled by the unresolved issue. Each month, the couple attended the board meeting to present their concerns about the church, including a list of what I was doing wrong as senior pastor. I protested to the board this was wrong and hurtful to me, but they said, "We have to let people have their say." I grew to dread going to board meetings.

Though the ministry continued to grow, our lives were in pain. Bitterness began to weaken our effectiveness. The joy of ministry was drained and attempts at reconciliation were unsuccessful, even with the assistance of a veteran pastor. Bitter resentment took root in our lives like a crop of weeds in a beautiful garden. But God was at work in our lives. (You'll read about the miraculous ending to this story later in the chapter.)

Resentment Fuel

Is life fair? If I had a dollar for every time I heard my two daughters protest, "It's not fair," I'd have a good start on a retirement fund. Perhaps it would have been simpler to shorten "It's not fair" to "INF," as in, "I did the dishes last night. INF." "She always gets to stay up late. INF." Joanne and I went to great lengths to equalize everything. How naïve! After several years of INF-negotiating, I finally wised up and said, "You're right. Life isn't fair. Deal with it."

My daughters were more right than they realized: *life is not fair*. Not every wrong will be made right, nor every injustice made equitable in this life. Many things simply aren't fair. Life comes packaged with

THE EDGE

plenty of "INF" stuff—resentment fuel. Who hasn't experienced one or more of these potential causes for resentment?

- An antagonist makes your life miserable.
- A promotion you deserved goes to someone else.
- Someone you thought was a friend stabs you in the back.
- An unscrupulous salesman talks you into an unwise purchase.
- Your marriage partner is unfaithful.
- A fabricated rumor circulates that damages your reputation.
- You do the work, but someone else gets the credit.
- You are maligned for taking a courageous stand for truth and justice.
- Your grown child no longer speaks with you.
- You are lied to.
- You work tirelessly at your job but get fired.
- A confidence is violated.
- You suffer a permanent injury from a driver who ran a red light.
- You attempt to help someone, and they turn against you.
- Money you're owed remains unpaid.
- A broken promise leaves you disappointed.

The Roots of Resentments

During their wilderness wandering, the Israelites came face to face with adversity that fueled resentment.

> *Now the people complained about their hardships in the hearing of the LORD, and when he heard them his anger was aroused. Then fire from the LORD burned among them and consumed some of the outskirts of the camp. When the people cried out to Moses, he prayed to the LORD and the fire died down. So that place was called Taberah, because fire from the LORD had burned among them. The rabble with them began to crave other food, and again the Israelites started wailing and said, "If only we had meat to eat! We remember the fish we ate in Egypt at no cost—also the cucumbers, melons, leeks, onions and garlic. But now we have lost our appetite; we never see anything but this manna!"* (Num. 11:1-6)

Resentment invaded the camp and gripped the people's attitudes. The *people complained about their hardships,* and resentment spread like flu in the pew. God's displeasure with their attitude was evident as fire from the LORD burned among them. The phrase is used in 1 Kings 18:38 to describe fire ignited by lightning. Whether it was lightning-caused or not, the fire that burned among them was disciplinary action from God. Despite the fire from God, their discontent still smoldered: "If only we had meat to eat!" they cried. Moses, discouraged by their bellyaching, went before God.

> *"Where can I get meat for all these people? They keep wailing to me, 'Give us meat to eat!' I cannot carry all these people by myself; the burden is too heavy for me. If this is how you are going to treat me, put me to death right now—if I have found favor in your eyes—and do not let me face my own ruin."* (Num. 11:13-15)

Resentment got a stranglehold on Moses as well. He complained that the burden was too heavy, and he submitted his resignation. His despondency was so deep, he asked God to take his life.

Adversity is only one type of resentment. Understanding the resentment's root issue will help release it. These four types get down to the root issues.

Type One: Resentment regarding life circumstances

You may feel that circumstances always bounce the wrong way for you. Questions similar to these may float in your mind:

- *How did I end up with a job I dislike?*
- *Why is it* always *my car that breaks down?*
- *I've been honest and hardworking, but I still can't pay my bills each month.*
- *Why am I sidelined with pain and poor health while my friends are active and healthy?*

Adversity, hardship, and wilderness-wandering were the initial resentments that gripped the Israelites, and God was clearly displeased

THE EDGE

when they complained about their hardships (Num. 11:1). Elsewhere in the Bible, God warns against a complaining attitude. James says, *Don't grumble against each other, brothers, or you will be judged. The Judge is standing at the door!* (James 5:9). Even though the Judge at the door refers to the Lord's return, I can't read this verse without imagining Jesus standing in the doorway of the room where I am as he listens in to my grumbling.

All of us experience days when we don't feel well—not enough sleep, a headache, allergies, flu-like symptoms. Since it's wrong to complain, does this mean you should pretend you're okay while your grumpy attitude tells everyone you're not? No. Instead, it's important to report what you're going through rather than faking it. Simply say, "I'm not feeling well today, and I could use some extra grace."

On the other hand, if someone continuously whines and moans about every ache and pain, people will find it depressing to be around them. Paul warned, *Do everything without complaining or arguing.* Then he explains why this is so important: *... so that you may become blameless and pure, children of God without fault in a crooked and depraved generation, in which you shine like stars in the universe* (Phil. 2:14-15). If you're known for constant complaining about work conditions, the weather, how unfair everyone is to you, the light of your Christian witness goes out. A complaining Christian is a contradiction; grumbling negates an effective witness to a lost world. A church with a lot of whining, complaining, and nitpicking will be highly ineffective at reaching people for Christ.

So what's the difference between *complaining* and *explaining*? This is the key distinction. *Complaining* drips with resentment; at the core, it's a bitter, unthankful attitude, ultimately toward God. *Explaining* an adversity is done with a grateful and joyful attitude. It's either "griping" or "gladness," "grumbling" or "gratefulness" in your attitude.

Day One Time Out

Power Thoughts for Your Time Alone with God

Complaining drips with resentment; at the core, it's a bitter, unthankful attitude toward God.

❏ What things are you are most likely to complain about? Did you grumble about something this week?

❏ Read James 5:7-18. Make some notes on what the passage says to do in various situations.

When you're suffering, be _____ like the farmer.
Don't _____ against each other, or you will be judged.
Don't _____ by heaven or earth or by anything else.
When you're in trouble, _____.
When you're happy, _____.
When you're sick, _____.
When you sin, confess your sins to _____.

❏ How will you apply this passage the next time you find reasons to complain?

❏ Let's consider a day when you didn't get enough sleep and feel achy all over. How would you express this to those around you without displaying an unthankful attitude toward God?

❏ Go to the back of your book and cut out or copy this week's meditation verse titled "Weed Killer for a Bitter Root." Carry it with you or put it someplace where you can direct your thoughts to it throughout the day and memorize it.

Type Two: Resentment against people who have hurt or disappointed you

We all have experienced hurt and pain from other people, and this type of resentment is usually deeper and more difficult to uproot. This may include being hurt by your parents or your children. Friends (or former friends) may have done things that brought deep pain into your life. They embarrassed you, made a caustic remark, betrayed you, put you down, and you live with the memory. The pain is deep and intensely personal.

An authority figure, such as an employer, school teacher, church leader, or law enforcement officer, may be a source of bitterness. One of my close friends was deeply hurt by a school teacher/coach who treated the athletes with special favors but ridiculed and picked on anyone who wasn't a jock. Another friend was falsely accused by his boss of stealing from the company. Even though he was exonerated of the charges, and it came to light that the boss lied because he felt threatened by the employee, this accusation ruined my friend's career in that field. In Numbers 11, Israel's complaints regarding adversity (Resentment Type One) also included resentment directed against Moses, the authority figure (Resentment Type Two).

Have you experienced the loss of a once close friend? Did a trusted friend turn against you? David had such an experience.

> *If an enemy were insulting me, I could endure it; if a foe were raising himself against me, I could hide from him. But it is you, a man like myself, my companion, my close friend, with whom I once enjoyed sweet fellowship as we walked with the throng at the house of God.* (Ps. 55:12-14)

This person was a former confidant, companion, and a close friend. David and this former friend worshiped God together. What went wrong in the relationship? We don't know the details, but David states this: *My companion attacks his friends; he violates his covenant. His speech is smooth as butter, yet war is in his heart; his words are more soothing than oil, yet they are drawn swords* (Ps. 55:20-21). This former friend was a back-stabbing betrayer. The pain ran deep. When your companion—

someone who was once your close friend—betrays you and stabs you in the back, remember Jesus felt the pain of Judas, the one who delivered him over to death.

If you've experienced this kind of loss, the closeness you once enjoyed in your relationship makes the loss sting even more. It's helpful to process this by writing a letter you never send. Describe what the person did and your feelings about it. You may want to read the letter to someone you can confide in and allow that person to help you process your feelings. Then tear up what you wrote. In some cases, you may want to write another letter that would be appropriate to send, explaining your sense of loss and seeking reconciliation.

Type Three: Resentment against yourself

You may resent senseless things you've done, your lack of resolve and will-power, or a foolish decision that brought great pain in your life. You may ask yourself questions similar to these:

- *Why do I yell at my kids?*
- *Why didn't I take better care of my body?*
- *Why did I foolishly blow all that money?*
- *Why do I always open my mouth when I know I should keep quiet?*

Paul's agony in Romans 7 is a self-directed type-three resentment: *I do not understand what I do. For what I want to do I do not do, but what I hate I do* (Rom. 7:15). Resentment against yourself and resentment of God are very similar; however, the cause of your self-resentment is usually something you had some degree of control over—your will was involved. The fourth type, God-resentment, which follows, is something you did *not* have control over.

Type Four: Resentment against God

Do you have questions similar to these?

- *Why am I afflicted with a debilitating disease while my godless neighbor enjoys robust health and great prosperity?*

- *Why did God make my nose crooked?*
- *Why was I born into a dysfunctional home?*
- *Why am I so average—nothing noteworthy to help me get ahead?*

The other three types of resentments—circumstances, people who wronged you, and yourself—often reflect this fourth underlying resentment, the granddaddy of them all: *resentment against God.* After all, *The LORD makes some poor and others rich; he brings some down and lifts others up* (1 Sam. 2:7 NLT). Many reject God or resist his control over their lives because deep down they feel God has given them a raw deal. Isaiah warns, *What sorrow awaits those who argue with their Creator? Does a clay pot argue with its maker? Does the clay dispute with the one who shapes it, saying, "Stop, you're doing it wrong!"* (Isa. 45:9 NLT). God takes responsibility for shaping you.

Each type of resentment often includes one or more of the other types. Moses got hit with all four types of resentments in this singular incident. Take another look at Numbers 11:13-15 in this paraphrase. Here we see that resentment simmering under the surface makes it difficult to trust God.

> *He prayed: I am your servant, LORD, so why are you doing this to me? What have I done to deserve this? You've made me responsible for all these people, but they're not my children. You told me to nurse them along and to carry them to the land you promised their ancestors. They keep whining for meat, but where can I get meat for them? This job is too much for me. How can I take care of all these people by myself? If this is the way you're going to treat me, just kill me now and end my miserable life!* (Num. 11:11-15 CEV)

While this is primarily a God-resentment, you will notice Moses had all four types as well.
1. Resentment of circumstances: *Where can I get meat for them?*

THE EDGE

2. Resentment of others: *They keep whining for meat.*

3. Resentment of self: *This job is too much for me.*

4. Resentment of God: *If this is the way you're going to treat me, just kill me now and end my miserable life!*

Moses isn't suicidal, but he is one step from it. When someone has unresolved resentment that includes all four levels, thoughts of suicide may invade their thinking.

Day Two Time Out

Power Thoughts for Your Time Alone with God

You intended to harm me, but God intended it for good to accomplish what is now being done, the saving of many lives. (Gen. 50:20)

❑ Read Genesis 37:19-36 and 50:18-20.

❑ Using the worksheet in Appendix D or a blank sheet of paper, do a personal inventory, including unfair circumstances, mistreatment by others, disappointments regarding yourself, or resentful feelings toward God. Make certain your list remains private. We will work more with this inventory later in the chapter.

❑ Put a 1, 2, 3, or 4 next to each resentment on your list to identify the type of resentment (resentments are often more than one type):

Type 1: Resentment of circumstances
Type 2: Resentment of others
Type 3: Resentment of yourself
Type 4: Resentment of God

❑ During your time of prayer, ask God to give you a Joseph perspective *(you intended to harm me, but God intended it for good)* regarding those who've hurt you.

Dave and Joanne Beckwith

The Caustic Effects of Resentments

Resentments work like a slow-acting poison, eating away at physical, mental, emotional, and spiritual health. When someone says, "If it's the last thing I do, I'll get even with that slime- ball," it may truly be the last thing they do. Many have dropped dead from a heart attack while brimming with resentment. A scoundrel of a guy named Nabal, whom the Bible describes as surly and mean, mistreated David and his men and then spent the night getting drunk. In the morning, he suffered a massive heart attack or stroke. Nabal's heart failed him, and he became like stone. His body was paralyzed, and he died ten days later (1 Sam. 25:37-38).

Resentments need a bold label that says, Warning: Toxic Poison. When David was filled with resentments and regrets, he said, *I'm on the edge of losing it—the pain in my gut keeps burning* (Ps. 38:17 MSG). These insidious thoughts attach to your mind and emotions, and they are "re-sent" (root of the word resentment)—played over and over again. This process of ruminating over resentments pollutes and poisons your inner being. *Watch out that no poisonous root of bitterness grows up to trouble you, corrupting many* (Heb. 12:15 NLT). The poison of resentment will inevitably seep from your life into the lives of others—your spouse, your children, your employees, your friends. Proverbs warns, *The fool who provokes his family to anger and resentment will finally have nothing worthwhile left. He shall be the servant of a wiser man* (Prov. 11:29 TLB).

The word "bitterness" is the Greek word *pikria,* which means "to cut, to prick." A bitter person often makes caustic, cutting comments. The Psalmist said regarding his bitter enemies, *See what they spew from their mouths—they spew out swords from their lips (Ps. 59:7).* I picture little, flashing daggers popping out when they speak. Rabbi Yehuda Berg stated, "Hurt people hurt people. That's how pain patterns get passed on, generation after generation after generation."[37] It's also true that hurt people hurt themselves. In a strange irony, when you resent someone, you may actually begin to resemble their behaviors and attitudes. Many with bitter resentment toward a parent have said, "I'll never be like my mom or dad." Ten years later, they're horrified to see their resemblance to the parent they despise. The caustic effects of resentment are 24/7—always with you unless released and healed.

THE EDGE

> The moment I start hating a man, I become his slave. I can't enjoy my work anymore because he even controls my thoughts. My resentments produce too many stress hormones in my body and I become fatigued after only a few hours of work. The work I formerly enjoyed is now drudgery. Even vacations cease to give me pleasure. ...
> The man I hate hounds me wherever I go. I can't escape his tyrannical grasp on my mind.[38]

While speaking at a camp for a week, I noticed a man about thirty years of age in the audience, listening very intently but with a noticeable and somewhat obnoxious facial twitch. The twitch was so pronounced I found it distracting while I spoke. After the session, he asked if he could speak with me. We sat down in the front of the chapel and talked until after midnight. His life was full of deep bitterness about his ex-wife and about an employer who let him go. I was feeling quite hopeless to assist him with all the brimming anger. Finally, about one a.m., I suggested we kneel together by a bench in the chapel and pray. He began to sob deeply as he asked God for forgiveness and to take away his resentment of his ex-wife and former employer. When we stood up, I put an arm on his shoulder, and I noticed the facial twitch had stopped. I didn't think too much about it, but the next morning at breakfast, I again noticed the absence of the twitch. Throughout the remainder of the week, the entire camp was astounded at the change in his appearance, the absence of the facial twitch, the smile on his face, and the change in his attitude. A year later, I spoke in the area again and asked about him. He was traveling, so I didn't get to see him, but the pastor assured me he was doing well, and the facial twitch had not returned. The twitch was likely related to *Tourette* syndrome, a condition characterized by eye-blinking, coughing, throat clearing, sniffing, and facial movements; causes include a variety of genetic and environmental factors. It would be erroneous to assume all cases of Tourette syndrome are caused by unresolved emotional issues. However, in this case, the pent-up bitterness and resentment were clearly the cause of the facial twitch.

Resentments are like the mercury in a thermometer, rising and then subsiding, depending on the heat and pressure in life. The resentment in the thermometer is toxic to the human system, a poison that can easily leak out and infect others. The only way to deal effectively with resentment is to drain the mercury from the thermometer. When this occurs, the outcome is the wonderful freedom of resentment-free living.

Day Three Time Out

Power Thoughts for Your Time Alone with God

Resentments work like a slow-acting poison eating away at physical, mental, emotional, and spiritual health.

- ❏ Think of a time when you were upset and resentful. How did this resentment affect your physical, mental, emotional, and spiritual health? How was your sleep affected?

- ❏ Read Hebrews 12:1-3, 14-15. Observation: your mind can be "fixed on Jesus" (verse 2) or "fixed on an all-consuming resentment" (verse 15). In your experience, how does one affect the other?

- ❏ Look again at verse 1. To change the focus of your mind to Jesus rather than your resentment, make this your prayer today.

"Lord, help me throw off everything that hinders and holds me back (my anger and resentments, feelings of failure and shame) and any sin that is currently entangling me and pulling me down. I am willing—set me free. Give me the strength to run with perseverance the race you have for me. Change my mental focus and allow me to fix my eyes on you, Jesus."

Breaking a Resentment Headlock

If you're expecting every wrong to be made right and every injustice to be made equitable in this life, you're in for a life of disappointment. Many things aren't fair and never will be in this lifetime. Everyone I know has suffered enough injustices and wrongs to remain bitter for their entire lifetime. They could crawl into a corner in a fetal position and feel sorry for themselves all their days. *A choice must be made: release resentments or remain mentally, emotionally, and spiritually crippled.* The sidelines of the game of life are lined with once effective, multi-talented, bitter people, now crippled with arthritic-like resentments.

Having personally wrestled with my own resentments and having worked with those gripped by them, I am convinced resentments are one of Satan's primary strongholds. Here are four crucial steps—steps you will use over and over again—to uproot resentments and be set free.

Step One: I am powerless to release my resentments.

Most people attempt to deal with resentments in one of two ways, neither of which work. One method is to bury the resentful feelings by telling yourself, *I'll ignore the pain, and it will go away sooner or later.* The other approach is to deny the hurt—put on your superman or superwoman cape, pretend to be invincible, and tell yourself, *I'm tough. They tried to hurt me, but there's no way they can get to me, and I'm not going to give them the satisfaction of thinking they can.* You may appear strong and confident, but you're simply suppressing the pain. Buried, unhealed resentments have long-term effects: broken relationships, distrust of others, a sour attitude, inability to be close, illicit sexual escapades, risk-taking, or a variety of pain-numbing behaviors like overeating, alcohol abuse, drug use, etc.

James 3:14 says, *If you harbor bitter envy ... do not boast about it or deny the truth.* Harboring bitter envy is carrying around a "boat load" of ugly feelings that are anchored in your soul. James goes on to identify the two ways mentioned above that most people use to deal with bitterness. One is to bury the resentment and pretend it doesn't exist—*deny the truth.* The other is to assume arrogantly it's no big deal, and you can handle it on your own—*boast about it.*

THE EDGE

Hopefully, no one has ever put a headlock on you (unless you're a competitive wrestler). This is a method of attacking and restraining someone by putting an arm around their head, usually at the neck. This method can cause death by asphyxiation if held long enough. Deep-rooted resentments are like a "mental headlock," exerting overwhelming control. You're in the grip, the stranglehold of something bigger and more powerful than you. To break the stranglehold and regain your edge, you must appropriate God's power. The first step to being set free begins with a prayer of surrender, a cry for help: "Lord Jesus, I'm powerless to break the stranglehold of my resentments."

Step Two: I'm willing for Jesus Christ to set me free from my resentments.

The key word is "willing." You've likely met people controlled by anger and resentments, but they don't want to let go. What will they have to talk about? They enjoy retelling the sordid details of all the times they've been wronged to anyone who will listen. They begin to display their resentments—how they carry themselves, their general demeanor, even the lines in their face. Their resentments become their identity.

Being "willing to release" a resentment is quite different from the "ability to release" a resentment, as I've discovered in counseling those with a deep-seated bitterness. I listen to them spill their story of someone who's hurt them deeply, and then they say, "I don't know if I'll ever be able to forgive this person. Every time I see them, the pain resurfaces. I've tried to forgive them, but I just can't let go of the hurt. I *can't* forgive them." First I respond by agreeing with them. "You're right. You can't forgive them. This is something beyond your ability, but don't despair. This is exactly where God wants you to be." Then I explain further. "I'm not asking if you're *able* to forgive them. I'm asking you if you're *willing* to forgive them." Finally they say, "Okay. I'm willing." This is the beginning of a breakthrough. Willingness is the second step—and a mandatory one—to be set free.

Step Three: I choose to allow God to right this wrong in his time.

Resentments are often rooted in some injustice. Something inside you screams for the wrong to be made right. Like a balance and a scale, a wrong tips the scale of justice, creating a driving need to balance the scale. This is why revenge, though wrong and destructive, seems so inviting.

Justice **Injustice**

When hurt, it's normal to want the wrong made right. Why? Justice needs to be done and the equilibrium of fairness restored. You may fear that the one who hurt you will get off without consequences. Letting go seems the most unnatural thing to do.

Most Bible scholars believe that as Paul wrote 2 Timothy, he was in the cold and filth of the Mamertine Prison in Rome, awaiting possible execution. I'll never forget the experience of visiting this prison, one of the oldest jails in the world, dating back some 2,500 years. The jail is constructed with an upper and lower level. Condemned prisoners were thrown into the circular lower room through a hole in the center of the upper-level floor. The lower section is solid granite, round and approximately thirteen feet in diameter and six and a half feet high. It has little light and air from the outside, and no sanitation. An iron door opens to a passageway that leads to the Tiber River. Many of the prisoners died from filth and disease while others died from strangulation or starvation. To dispose of a body, guards opened the iron door and dumped it into the passageway that emptied into the river.[39]

In the darkness of this filthy hole, Paul wrote his "swan song," the last words we have from this great apostle. We don't know if he was executed or if he was released and later traveled to Spain. What we do know is that he expected to be put to death. In the fourth chapter of 2 Timothy, Paul remembered those who deserted him, and in particular that no one supported him when he was on trial. Paul's heart of forgiveness is evident when he says, *May it not be held against them* (4:16). He also remembered the injuries inflicted on him by a man named Alexander, and though he didn't mention the offense, Paul was deeply hurt. *Alexander the metalworker did me a great deal of harm. The Lord will repay him for what he has done* (2 Tim. 4:14). Paul responded in two ways, both very important. *First, he acknowledged the personal injury.* Paul didn't try to play tough by pretending it was no big deal. It hurt, and he admitted to being wounded. This is crucial to effectively process a resentment. *Second, he assigned to God the responsibility for making it right.* He put this on "God's To-Do List" by saying, *the Lord will repay him for what he has done.* In 1 Timothy 1:20, Paul mentions an Alexander, who was disciplined and turned over to Satan. This may be the same person though we can't be certain of this.

On occasion, revenge has raced through my mind, and though I knew it was wrong, it was enticing. With God's prompting, rather than responding with revenge, I did what Paul did, inserting the name of the person in the verse and asking the Lord to repay: _____
did me a great deal of harm. The Lord will repay them for what they have done.

When I've surrendered a point of resentment, I've sometimes seen God bring astounding repayment into the person's life within a relatively short period of time. To our surprise, one couple who'd hurt Joanne and me came to us to apologize. God allowed them to experience precisely what they did to us, and through this, they realized the pain they'd caused. In other situations, I know God is at work making things right though it isn't evident to me how he's doing it. Bottom line: *put the repayment of a wrong done to you on "God's To-Do List" and leave it there.*

Step Four: I yield my resentments to Christ and choose to forgive those who've wronged me.

Feel the pain, acknowledge the hurt, and ask Christ to heal the deepest resentment in your heart. As you pray, allow him to bring to mind your own weaknesses and failures. Confess your sins and the pain you've brought *to* others, as you receive Christ's healing for the pain inflicted by others. Visualize yourself there with Christ on the cross, identified in his suffering: *He personally carried our sins in his body on the cross so that we can be dead to sin and live for what is right. By his wounds you are healed* (1 Pet. 2:24 NLT). In the nail-scarred hands of Christ, we find healing.

    Forgiveness is primarily a choice of your will rather than a feeling. From a human standpoint, forgiveness is extremely difficult if not impossible. The power to forgive comes from Christ's forgiveness of your sins. Forgiveness is not forgetting the incidents—it's releasing those involved. Forgiving and being forgiven are inseparable. *For if you forgive men when they sin against you, your heavenly Father will also forgive you. But if you do not forgive men their sins, your Father will not forgive your sins* (Matt. 6:14-15). Forgiveness doesn't wait for others to acknowledge their wrong and apologize, as they may never own up to the hurt they caused. When you forgive, *you're* the one set free.

Day Four Time Out
Power Thoughts for Your Time Alone with God

Forgiveness is primarily a choice of your will rather than a feeling.

- ❏ Read Ephesians 4:25-32.
- ❏ Pray through each of the four steps to release the resentments you wrote down on Day Two.

Apply Step One: I'm powerless to release my resentments. Pray through the resentments on your list, recognizing you are powerless to deal with these yourself. Ask him to break the "mental headlock."

Apply Step Two: I'm willing for Jesus Christ to set me free from my resentments. Go over each resentment on your list and pray, "Lord, I'm willing to release this resentment." Put a "W" next to each resentment to indicate this moment of willingness and surrender.

Apply Step Three: I choose to allow God to right this wrong in his time. Paul was deeply hurt when he wrote, *Alexander the metalworker did me a great deal of harm. The Lord will repay him for what he has done* (2 Tim. 4:14). Take the two steps Paul did. First, he *acknowledged the personal injury,* and second, he *assigned to God the responsibility* for making it right. Acknowledge the pain when someone hurts you. Assign to God the responsibility to deal with the issue. Insert the name of the person who did you harm. _____ *did me a great deal of harm. The Lord will repay them for what they have done.* Once you've completed this, put the initials "GTDL" next to each resentment of a person who has wronged you. This indicates it is now on "God's To-Do List." Remember that forgiving isn't a feeling—it's a choice.

Apply Step Four: I yield my resentments to Christ and choose to forgive those who've wronged me. With every resentment on your list, pray this prayer: "I yield this resentment to you, Lord. I remember how much you've forgiven me. As you've forgiven me, and by the power of your forgiveness, I choose to forgive this person. Thank you for setting me free from the power of this resentment." When you've completed this, you may want to tear the list up and dispose of it.

NOTE: Repeat these four steps as often as necessary.

Dave and Joanne Beckwith

What about Reconciliation?

It's wonderful when reconciliation takes place. Certainly pray for reconciliation, and be willing to do your part to bring it about. However, reconciliation may not take place, or it may be delayed many years.

Despite several meetings with the couple mentioned at the start of this chapter, reconciliation did not occur. Three years later, God led us to Southern California. Joanne and I worked through forgiveness, and by God's grace, we moved forward.

Fast-forward seventeen years to 2001. A Sunday was designated as World Reconciliation Day, when believers were encouraged to make restitution, apologize for hurts, and seek to be at peace with one another. Pastors around the world were encouraged to speak on the subject of reconciliation, and I prepared a message on the topic.

As I stood up to speak on reconciliation, I was stunned. Sitting in the fourth or fifth row was the couple who'd inflicted such pain in our lives seventeen years earlier. What were they doing here? They lived nearly 500 miles away, and I couldn't imagine why they'd be in the congregation that day. I certainly didn't want to see them. Even though I'd forgiven them, the strong feelings of hurt and resentment surged through my mind, making it difficult to continue speaking. Knowing they were in the building opened up old wounds and triggered painful memories from the past. Meanwhile, Joanne was feeling her own pain, as this couple was sitting in her row, a few seats away.

I struggled to continue. How could I speak of reconciliation while simultaneously fighting a fierce battle with the issue? This was too close for comfort—too personal. Finally, while delivering the message, I prayed silently, "Lord, I'm willing for reconciliation." Immediately I had the freedom to continue and complete the message.

Later we discovered the couple was visiting Southern California, and they chose a church from the Yellow Pages. God arranged for them to come to Woodbridge Community Church not knowing I was the senior pastor. They were as shocked as we were when they walked in and saw I was the pastor of the church and the speaker for the morning.

Following the service, Joanne and I talked with the couple, and God brought about a spirit of reconciliation. Who but God could have arranged this miraculous meeting on World Reconciliation Sunday more than seventeen years after the conflict?

THE EDGE

Two reminders stand out from this God-arranged meeting. First, be ready for reconciliation: sometimes when you least expect it, God will provide an opportunity to bring healing to the relationship. You may see the person in the grocery store or unexpectedly at a wedding. Don't hide or pretend you don't see them. Greet them, and breathe a prayer: "Lord, I'm willing to be reconciled." Be willing to acknowledge your wrongs, and let God take it from there.

Second, resentments that you've dealt with years earlier can resurface. Forgiveness is a lot like peeling an onion, layer after layer, forgiving again and again, and you may shed tears as you peel each layer of the onion. Repeat these four steps as often as needed, daily if necessary.

- Step One: I'm powerless to release my resentments.
- Step Two: I'm willing for Jesus Christ to set me free from my resentments.
- Step Three: I choose to allow God to right this wrong in his time.
- Step Four: I yield my resentments to Christ and choose to forgive those who've wronged me.

By choosing to forgive, do you forget the details of the wrong or injustice? No. In most cases, you'll continue to remember the incident. As Jesus Christ brings healing to your life, the day will come when the stinger is removed, the bitterness is absent, and the poison is no longer in your life. One of the famous survivors of the Holocaust, Corrie Ten Boom, wisely stated, "Forgiveness is to set a prisoner free, and to realize that the prisoner was you."

Carrying around a load of bitterness and resentment isn't an indicator of a strong person; it's a sign of weakness, a disabling limp in life. It takes a strong person to forgive. And only God can give you the power to forgive, to turn a debilitating weakness into a display of his strength in your life.

Day Five Time Out
Power Thoughts for Your Time Alone with God
Forgiveness is a lot like peeling an onion, layer after layer, forgiving again and again, and you may shed tears as you peel each layer of the onion.

❑ What resentment do you find most difficult to release? Ask God to work within you to be willing to forgive.

❑ Read Matthew 6:9-15.

❑ Notice that "being forgiven" of your sins requires your willingness to "forgive others" (verse 12).

❑ Further, notice that "not yielding to temptation" and "being rescued from the evil one" (verse 13) are preceded and followed by your willingness to forgive others (vv. 12, 14-15). In what ways are you more vulnerable to temptation when you're holding on to resentment?

❑ Pray through the Lord's Prayer one phrase at a time.

Our Father in heaven, may your name be kept holy. May your Kingdom come soon. May your will be done on earth, as it is in heaven. Give us today the food we need, and forgive us our sins, as we have forgiven those who sin against us. And don't let us yield to temptation, but rescue us from the evil one. If you forgive those who sin against you, your heavenly Father will forgive you. But if you refuse to forgive others, your Father will not forgive your sins (Matt. 6:9-15 NLT).

STRENGTH TEAM

SESSION FOUR

RELEASING RESENTMENTS

Most people attempt to deal with resentments in one of two ways, neither of which works. One method is to bury the resentful feelings by telling yourself, *I'll ignore the pain, and it'll go away sooner or later.* The other approach is to deny the hurt—put on your superman or superwoman cape, pretend to be invincible, and tell yourself, *I'm tough. They tried to hurt me, but there's no way they can get to me, and I'm not going to give them the satisfaction of thinking they can.* In this session, we're going to discover a radically different way to deal with resentments. You'll have the opportunity to walk through four life-changing steps to be set free. Let's get started!

CONNECT

❑ What ticks you off? What are you prone to complain about? Are these triggers the same or different? Do you have a "pet peeve"?

GROW

❑ As a group, read 2 Timothy 4:9-18. Confined in prison, Paul had ample cause to be bitter and resentful. Identify in this passage several things that were potential sources of bitterness for Paul and discuss how he applied a God-perspective. Write them on a poster board and discuss them as a group.

> *Timothy, please come as soon as you can. Demas has deserted me because he loves the things of this life and has gone to Thessalonica. Crescens has gone to Galatia, and Titus has gone to Dalmatia. Only Luke is with me. Bring Mark with you when you come, for he will be helpful to me in my ministry. I sent Tychicus to Ephesus. When you come, be sure to bring the coat I left with Carpus at Troas. Also bring my books, and especially my papers. Alexander the coppersmith did me much harm, but the Lord will judge him for what he has done. Be careful of him, for he fought against everything we said.*

THE EDGE

The first time I was brought before the judge, no one came with me. Everyone abandoned me. May it not be counted against them. But the Lord stood with me and gave me strength so that I might preach the Good News in its entirety for all the Gentiles to hear. And he rescued me from certain death. Yes, and the Lord will deliver me from every evil attack and will bring me safely into his heavenly Kingdom. All glory to God forever and ever! Amen. (2 Tim. 4:9-18 NLT)

(If some of the names are too difficult to pronounce, substitute the name with something like "Mr. C" or "Mr. T" or something similar.)

APPLY

- Love "keeps no record of wrongs" according to 1 Corinthians 13:5. To assist with understanding what this means in practical terms, think through your answer to each of these statements and have fun discussing them as a group.

    1. My "record of wrongs" is erased when someone asks to be forgiven, but not until then.

        Agree   Disagree

    2. My "record of wrongs" is effectively eliminated by overlooking the pain and minimizing the hurt.

        Agree   Disagree

    3. Keeping "no record of wrongs" means the relationship is restored.

        Agree   Disagree

    4. Keeping "no record of wrongs" means forgetting the offense.

        Agree   Disagree

    5. Holding on to a resentment makes me more vulnerable to temptation.

        Agree   Disagree

- ❑ Have you experienced victory in forgiving someone? If so, please share it with the group.

- ❑ Read aloud in unison the "Changing My Mind" verse below.

> **Weed Killer for a Bitter Root**
> *Look after each other so that none of you fails to receive the grace of God. Watch out that no poisonous root of bitterness grows up to trouble you, corrupting many.* (Heb. 12:15 NLT)
> 🕊 **Changing My Mind – Week 4**

- ❑ Discuss how you can look after each other to prevent bitterness.

PRAY

- ❑ Commit to remind each other to walk through the steps whenever resentments surface. Close by praying these four steps one at a time. Have someone in the group read Step One, and then spend a brief time in silent prayer, allowing each person to apply this. Then proceed with the other steps, with silent prayer after each one.

  - Step One: I'm powerless to release my resentments.
  - Step Two: I'm willing for Jesus Christ to set me free from my resentments.
  - Step Three: I choose to allow God to right this wrong in his time.
  - Step Four: I yield my resentments to Christ and choose to forgive those who've wronged me.

It's quite common that one or more individuals in the group may have difficulty releasing resentments. Don't rush the process. As a group, you can gather around them for special prayer, but don't push for or expect

THE EDGE

an instant release of resentments. Some hurts are very deep; patience and willingness to let them go will bring healing in God's time.

SHARE

❑ Most people like sharing their opinion or expressing what bothers them. Look for an opportunity to start a conversation with someone this week. At an appropriate moment, ask the person a discussion starter like this:

- *What ticks you off? What ignites your fuse?*
- *How do you handle it when someone does you wrong?*
- *Why do some people hold on to resentments while others release them and move on?*
- *What's the key to releasing a resentment?*

❑ Look for an opportunity to explain how Jesus Christ set you free from your resentment.

CHAPTER FIVE
RELEASING REGRETS

The prison door to the jail cell of regrets has flung open.
Walk out, walk free.

- *If only I hadn't said ...*
- *If only I'd been there for ...*
- *If only I hadn't responded the way I did when ...*
- *If only I hadn't done what I did ...*
- *If only I'd paid attention when ...*

If you're alive, you inevitably have regrets. Each of us has something we wish we could do over in a different way. The "if only ..." tape plays over and over again in your mind as a reminder of what could have been, what should have been. Your past drains joy from the present. Living with unresolved regrets is like trying to swim tangled in seaweed. Some regrets are secret, and you may be thinking, *If others knew what I know about me, I'd be finished.* Regrets are chains of self-berating. While resentments have to do with others and forgiving them, regrets have to do with ourselves and accepting God's forgiveness. Regrets and resentments are the ball and chain of an immobilized person.

God never intended that you live your life on a guilt trip, burdened with unresolved regrets. He provides the resources for regret-free living. It's a promise. Living regret-free doesn't mean your memory is erased; instead, the regret no longer controls you and holds you back. You no longer beat yourself up over what happened. Properly processed, regrets have the potential to become high-powered motivation for stronger faith, achievement, and compassion for others. Regrets are a weakness that can be turned into a great strength—his power point in your life.

Types of Regrets

I group regrets into three types: 1) embarrassing; 2) painful; and 3) sinful. Of course, there's overlap between the types, which will become obvious.

Embarrassing Regrets

Have any of these things happened to you? Falling on the way to the platform to make a presentation, losing your car in the parking lot, asking a woman who's gained weight when she's expecting, splitting your pants in public, walking into the wrong restroom, falling out of your seat while dozing off in church, getting the hiccups during your wedding ceremony. I'm certain you can add a few.

If you've failed a driver's test, you may not want to tell the world about it, but take heart— you're probably ahead of this driver. Mrs. Beatrice Park was nervous while taking her fifth driving test. As her foot hit the accelerator instead of the clutch, the car shot forward off the embankment and into the river below. She and the examiner climbed out of the vehicle and waited on the roof to be rescued by helicopter. In a state of shock, the examiner was sent home, still clutching his clipboard. After being rescued, Mrs. Park asked if she'd passed her driving test. She was told, "We can't say until we've seen the examiner's report."[40]

Painful Regrets

This type of regret isn't necessarily sinful, but it may bring dire consequences and long-term grief. A split-second decision in traffic that injures or kills another person can produce a haunting regret. Making an unwise business decision can have far-reaching ramifications—loss of money, business, home, and family security. Rehearsing what you should have done differently becomes a relentless obsession. These regrets are agonizing; ideals shatter as disappointment replaces dreams.

THE EDGE

Sinful Regrets

Many, if not most, of our regrets are sinful choices that leave a trail of sorrow and disappointment. Of course, sinful regrets usually include the other two types—sin is embarrassing as well as painful. Sin comes packaged with slick advertising, but underneath it's a big lie, a lie that seduces our cravings and our pride. David's sin, examined in the next section, is a vivid picture of sinful regrets.

Dealing with Regrets: What Doesn't Work

Rationalizing or burying regrets may seem like the best strategy to quiet the ghosts of your past. However, no matter how tightly you bolt the door of your memories, the regrets rattle in the closet. They color thinking, imparting a defeatist attitude and a loser's limp and making it more difficult to grow in your Christian faith. You've probably attempted to deal with regrets in one or both of these ways.

Berating Yourself

Depending on the severity of the disappointment, self-berating may become a regular occurrence. The recording plays over and over again: *I'm no good. I'm horrible. I'm despicable. How could I have done what I did?* When a believer becomes overwhelmed with feelings of failure, Satan has won a strategic battle. C. S. Lewis said, "Moral collapse follows upon spiritual collapse," and another person said, "It is Satan's strategy to get a Christian preoccupied with their failures; from then on the battle is won."[41]

David journals his inner turmoil and the physical and emotional impact of his sin in this Psalm.

> *[4] My guilt has overwhelmed me like a burden too heavy to bear. [5] My wounds fester and are loathsome because of my sinful folly. [6] I am bowed down and brought very low; all day long I go about mourning. [7] My back is filled with searing pain; there is no health in my body. [8] I am feeble and utterly crushed; I groan in anguish of heart. [9] All my longings lie open before you, O Lord; my sighing is not hidden from you. [10] My heart pounds, my strength fails me; even the light has gone from my eyes.* (Psalm 38:4-10)

David identified his regrets as a burden too heavy to bear, a highly toxic torment in his body, mind, and spirit. Psychologists and physicians call physical illness caused by mental conditions "psychosomatic illness." Often the cause is deeper. I call it "sin-somatic sickness." While sin does not cause most illnesses, some illnesses and mental conditions are a direct result of sin. From David's lament in Psalm 38, we find potential physical, spiritual, mental, and emotional consequences of unresolved regrets:

Symptoms of Sin-somatic Sickness

- Feeling overwhelmed (v. 4)
- Festering emotional wounds (v. 5)
- Depression—feeling low (v. 6)
- Mourning (v. 6)
- Searing back pain (v. 7)
- Loss of health (v. 7)
- Feebleness (v. 8)
- Feeling crushed (v. 8)
- Groaning (v. 8)
- Heart palpitations (v. 10)
- Failing strength (v. 10)
- Tired looking eyes, with the sparkle gone (v. 10)

Though the specific occasion for this Psalm is uncertain, the sin-somatic symptoms may well describe David's condition in the year that followed his sin with Bathsheba. David lusted for Bathsheba when he saw her bathing. His lust led to adultery, and she became pregnant. In an attempt to cover up the pregnancy, he called her husband, Uriah, home from the battlefield to sleep with his wife. Being a disciplined soldier, Uriah declined this opportunity the first night. The second night, David got him drunk, thinking he would surely go home and have sexual

THE EDGE

relations with his wife. When this failed, he arranged for Uriah's death on the battlefield. (You can read about it 2 Samuel 11—12.) It was lust, adultery, cover-up, deceit, and murder—and he knew it. That's a heavy load to be hauling around. I don't know what regrets are stuffed away in the closet of your mind, but if David could be set free from his regrets, then there's healing for the stuff that plagues your mind too.

Unresolved regrets will take you down. You get clobbered at the point of your greatest vulnerability. You find yourself on the mat, knocked out, down for the count, wondering what hit you. It's like professional boxer Ralph Walton, who was knocked out in ten and a half seconds in a boxing match in Lewiston, Maine. When the bell rang to begin the first round, his opponent, Al Couture, darted across the ring and swung at Walton before he'd left his corner. The ten and a half seconds included the ten seconds while he was counted out. Ralph was on his feet for a grand total of one-half second. With unresolved regrets, when a big challenge and a unique opportunity comes up, you may be knocked out of action before you know what hit you.

Day One Time Out

Power Thoughts for Your Time Alone with God

Living with unresolved regrets is like trying to swim tangled in seaweed.

- ❏ In your own words, describe what it's like to live with an unresolved regret.

- ❏ Read the account of David in 2 Samuel 11:1-27.

- ❏ What does this statement mean to you? "I don't know what regrets are stuffed away in the closet of your mind, but if David could be set free from his regrets, then there's healing for the stuff you regret too."

- ❏ Go to the back of your book and cut out or copy the meditation verse for this week titled "Blameless." Carry it with you or put it where you can direct your thoughts to it throughout the day as you memorize the verse.

Blaming Others

The "shame game"—berating yourself—is different from the "blame game"—berating others. A blaming person is often unaware of their critical spirit though it is painfully obvious to others. Those close bear the brunt of the blame: a sharp, cutting tongue, subtle putdowns, a bitter spirit. The Psalmist observed, *Your mouth is filled with wickedness, and your tongue is full of lies. You sit around and slander your brother—your own mother's son* (Ps. 50:19-20 NLT).

If your regrets weigh heavily on your conscience, you'll be prone to offset this by blaming others. Strangely, the flaws of others provide temporary mental relief from personal failures and disappointments. Guilt and blame work like a scale in your soul. When you feel guilty, the natural tendency is to be critical of others; blaming them seems to help in restoring the equilibrium. St. Augustine fessed up when he said, "O Lord, deliver me from this lust of always vindicating myself." It's the art of excusing ourselves by blaming the other person—something we inherited from our great grandparents, Adam and Eve.

It's a whole lot easier to blame others when they've wronged you. The more you blame, the less guilty you feel. Blame, blame, blame, and you fail to see your own wrongs. Jesus identified this in one of his great stories. The crowd must have gone hysterical with the humorous hyperbole in this warning about being judgmental:

> *"Do not judge, or you too will be judged. For in the same way you judge others, you will be judged, and with the measure you use, it will be measured to you. Why do you look at the speck of sawdust in your brother's eye and pay no attention to the plank in your own eye? How can you say to your brother, 'Let me take the speck out of your eye,' when all the time there is a plank in your own eye? You hypocrite, first take the plank out of your own eye, and then you will see clearly to remove the speck from your brother's eye."* (Matt. 7:1-5)

Use your imagination with this scene. This guy is walking around with an enormous plank sticking out of his eye. Meandering through life, he hauls this big piece of timber around, banging into things and looking weird to everyone. What does the world look like for "Mr. Log-in-the-eye"? It looks like a gigantic forest. What's in his eye is all he can see. Everywhere he turns, he sees wood, timber, logs. No wonder the speck in the other person's eye looks like an enormous log. Personal guilt magnifies the faults of others, distorting them all out of perspective. The apostle Paul cautioned,

> *You, therefore, have no excuse, you who pass judgment on someone else, for at whatever point you judge the other, you are condemning yourself, because you who pass judgment do the same things.* (Rom. 2:1)

I'm grateful to my parents for many things they imparted to me, including hard work, honesty, and moral values. On the flip side, my childhood home was a highly toxic and unhealthy emotional environment. Anger, hostility, and fights were frequent events for the eighteen years I lived at home. Many nights I went to sleep listening to the latest Mom-Dad fight getting out of control upstairs. It would go on for a half-hour or more, and then I'd hear the physical pushing, shoving, and hitting.

When I was in seventh grade, I got in the middle of a fight involving my dad and mom. He pushed her, and she fell. I jumped in, and Dad turned on me. I headed for the stairs to the basement, and he continued after me with his belt swinging wildly. One of the blows caused me to fall down the stairs and land on the concrete floor where I ended up bleeding and bruised. I ran from the house and found some cigarettes and started smoking. Somehow smoking numbed the seething anger. Most kids start smoking as a social dare, something they do to be cool and fit in with the crowd. For me, this was never the case. When I smoked, I was always alone and isolated in rage and resentment. This was the era of the "dirty five Christian don'ts": don't go to movies, drink alcohol, play cards, dance, or smoke. To me, smoking was worse than all the others. The result was agonizing shame, but when the anger and pain became too much, I resorted to numbing it. This continued off and on in the years that followed. Even though it was a rare occurrence, it was a deep regret and something I hoped no one would ever know. This led to hypocrisy and dishonesty, which was probably worse. For me, this was a deep-seated regret, loaded with shame, embarrassment, and disappointment. The easy thing to do would be to blame my parents, but this behavior was my own responsibility.

Day Two Time Out

Power Thoughts for Your Time Alone with God

"O Lord, deliver me from this lust of always vindicating myself." Augustine

❏ Identify when you've played the blame game. What was going on inside you?

❏ Read 1 Timothy 1:12-20. Paul describes himself as a blasphemer, persecutor, a violent man, and the worst of sinners. Paul was a terrorist before coming to Christ, and the searing memory of putting Christians to death must never have left his mind. Christ's complete forgiveness transformed Paul's life, and it will transform yours as well.

❏ You'll find it helpful to write down your regrets so they can be processed and released. Be specific. Identify actions, attitudes, words spoken, or things you failed to do. Use the Releasing Regrets (Appendix E) in the back of the book or a separate sheet of paper you can destroy later.

Dave and Joanne Beckwith

Dealing with Regrets: What Works

The word "agree" is a crucial word in dealing with regrets. It means to "bring something or someone into agreement; to harmonize, to reconcile." God wants you to be reconciled with him, to harmonize your relationship, to establish an agreement or understanding. There are four aspects to this God-agreement, the source of regret-free living.

1. Agree with God about your regrets.

Listen as God speaks.

- *Come, let's talk this over, says the Lord; no matter how deep the stain of your sins, I can take it out and make you as clean as freshly fallen snow. Even if you are stained as red as crimson, I can make you white as wool!* (Isa. 1:18 TLB)
- *He who conceals his sins does not prosper, but whoever confesses and renounces them finds mercy.* (Prov. 28:13)
- *I confess my sins; I am deeply sorry for what I have done.* (Ps. 38:18 NLT)
- *If we confess our sins, he is faithful and just and will forgive us our sins and purify us from all unrighteousness.* (1 John 1:9)

Don't rush past these verses. I suggest reading them again to get the full impact. Express your willingness to agree with your Creator. *You're right, God. I blew it. I sinned. I messed up. I was wrong. I failed.* The Greek word for "confess" in 1 John 1:9 means to "say the same thing as" or "agree with." Distress that drives us to God is for our benefit. *It turns us around. It gets us back in the way of salvation. We never regret that kind of pain. But those who let distress drive them away from God are full of regrets, and end up on a deathbed of regrets* (2 Cor. 7:10 MSG).

Sins are forgiven at the moment of salvation, but sinful behavior breaks fellowship with God. Confession is agreeing with God and seeking a new direction, thus renewing the intimacy of our relationship. Some assume confessing sin requires shedding tears and becoming emotionally distraught. This may occur, but it's not required to simply agree with God.

2. Agree with God regarding those you've hurt.

Jesus said if you come to offer your gift in worship and remember someone has something against you, be reconciled with that person first and then come and offer your gift.

> *So when you offer your gift to God at the altar, and you remember that your brother or sister has something against you, leave your gift there at the altar. Go and make peace with that person, and then come and offer your gift.* (Matt. 5:23-24 NCV)

The key phrase is "you remember that your brother or sister has something against you." Who do you need to be reconciled with? Your spouse, your parents or children, someone in the workplace, a neighbor? The verse says, "Go and make peace." This is a straightforward command. Go immediately and say, "I was wrong when I _____, and I want to ask for your forgiveness. Will you forgive me?" If you defrauded the person, make restitution by repaying what was stolen. Be careful not to indict the other person by blaming them in your apology. Don't say, "I'm sorry I yelled at you, but you made me so angry when you made that statement." Simply state the wrong: "I was wrong to yell at you. Please forgive me."

Zacchaeus had a life of regrets to deal with when he came to Jesus. He was a chief tax collector in the region of Jericho, and he'd become very rich cheating people. Tax collectors were considered traitors since they served the Roman government, and they were notorious for their dishonesty. As a result, they were expelled from the synagogue, and they couldn't serve as witnesses or as judges. They epitomized the term "filthy rich"—and they were despised.

When Jesus visited Jericho, short-of-stature Zacchaeus climbed a sycamore-fig tree to see Jesus over the crowd. Since he was considered to be a traitor, people in the crowd probably didn't want to associate with this slime anyway. I would imagine if he were among the crowd, someone would have jabbed him hard in the ribs, stepped on his toes, or given him a push. Jesus saw Zacchaeus up in the tree and announced he was going to his house that day. A remarkable change took place in Zacchaeus. The Scripture says, *Zacchaeus stood before the Lord and said, "I will give half my wealth to the poor, Lord, and if I have cheated people on their taxes, I will give them back four times as much!"* (Luke 19:8 NLT).

After his encounter with Jesus, I can imagine a Jewish family seeing Zacchaeus coming up the road to their house. "Oh, no! Here comes that blood-sucking tax collector to get money out of us and cheat us again." Zacchaeus knocks on the door and says, "Sorry to bother you, but I'm here with your tax refund. I'm returning the amount I cheated you out of, and I'm including 400 percent interest on the amount as well. Have a nice day." The reaction must have been astounding—dropped jaws, fainting spells, total disbelief. Who knows? Once they recovered from the shock, they may have invited Zach in for supper with the family. Zacchaeus was being set free from his regretful life.

When you ask forgiveness from another person, you have an impact on their "guilt-blame" balance. They may have been justifying their actions by blaming you. When you humble yourself and ask forgiveness, they suddenly become aware of their wrong in the situation. Don't count on it, but it's not uncommon for them to respond, "I was wrong as well. I ask your forgiveness for my part in this." This sort of action leads to the sweetness of reconciliation.

What if the other person doesn't have something against you? Years ago, Joanne felt she was obligated to apologize for negative thoughts she had about another girl. The girl didn't have a clue that Joanne felt this way about her so when Joanne apologized, the girl was shocked and hurt. If what you have to confess may be more hurtful than helpful, check with someone you trust before proceeding. Should a man tell a woman who is totally unaware of his thoughts, "I confess having lustful thoughts about you"? No!

Day Three Time Out

Power Thoughts for Your Time Alone with God

Cling to your faith in Christ, and keep your conscience clear. For some people have deliberately violated their consciences; as a result, their faith has been shipwrecked. (1 Tim. 1:19 NLT)

❏ Read Matthew 5:23-24 and Acts 16:24.

❏ Ask God to bring to mind people you've wronged. If these aren't on your list of regrets you wrote on day two, add them now. Take steps now to contact these people—in person, by phone, or if necessary, in a letter—and humbly ask, "Will you forgive me?" Put a check in the "apology" column when you've completed this.

3. Agree with God regarding his forgiveness.

You've likely heard someone say, "You need to forgive yourself." Is this biblical? Is it humanly possible?

I wish I had the name of the woman I met at a conference who challenged my thinking on this point. At the breakfast table, when the topic of forgiving yourself came up, she asked, "Is it humanly possible to forgive yourself?" I didn't reply immediately sensing she had an insight to share. She stated her opinion that, in most cases, forgiving yourself is humanly impossible. My mind immediately began to think through verses on the subject. *Hmm ... Is there a verse in the Bible that tells me to forgive myself?* I couldn't think of one, but the Scripture does say to forgive your enemies. So if you're your own worst enemy, I guess that would include forgiving yourself.

As I thought about her point, I realized this is where people get stuck. They try to forgive themselves, but they discover the harder they try, the deeper the feelings of regret. Forgiveness requires God's intervention. Rather than struggling to forgive yourself, agree with God and accept his forgiveness. If God—the Creator of the Universe, the ultimate judge of all, the one who night and day is surrounded by angels saying, "Holy, holy, holy is the LORD God Almighty"—chooses to forgive you, then who are you to doubt what he has done? Accept his forgiveness. This is the *only* way to appropriate true forgiveness of yourself. How could we possibly come before God's throne if our sins weren't totally forgiven? Trying to forgive yourself is a human effort of the flesh—futile and incomplete. Accepting God's forgiveness as your forgiveness is an act of faith, and without faith it's impossible to please God (Heb. 11:6).

God not only forgives, but he also forgets. *For I will forgive their wickedness and will remember their sins no more* (Jer. 31:34). What? How could God forget? Is God absent-minded or forgetful? No. He *chooses* to forget, to remember your sins no more. Max Lucado said it this way: "God doesn't just forgive, he forgets. He erases the board. He destroys the evidence. He burns the microfilm. He clears the computer. He doesn't remember my mistakes."[42]

Because you're in Christ, God accepts you as blameless, without a single fault (Eph. 1:4). Christ died for you that he might *present you holy in his sight, without blemish and free from accusation* (Col. 1:22). Hebrews 4:16 tells us, *Let us then approach the throne of grace with*

THE EDGE

confidence, so that we may receive mercy and find grace to help us in our time of need. If God hadn't forgiven and forgotten your failings, how could you come into his holy presence?

God's forgiveness as well as his choice not to remember your sins is woven throughout the Scriptures. Allow these verses to grip you:

- *For as high as the heavens are above the earth, so great is his love for those who fear him; as far as the east is from the west, so far has he removed our transgressions from us.* (Psalm 103:11-12)
- *Surely it was for my benefit that I suffered such anguish. In your love you kept me from the pit of destruction; you have put all my sins behind your back.* (Isa. 38:17)
- *Once again you will have compassion on us. You will trample our sins under your feet and throw them into the depths of the ocean!* (Mic. 7:19 NLT)
- *"I, even I, am he who blots out your transgressions, for my own sake, and remembers your sins no more."* (Isa. 43:25)
- *Repent, then, and turn to God, so that your sins may be wiped out, that times of refreshing may come from the Lord.* (Acts 3:19)
- *My dear children, I write this to you so that you will not sin. But if anybody does sin, we have one who speaks to the Father in our defense—Jesus Christ, the Righteous One.* (1 John 2:1)

Does your memory of a regrettable behavior disappear? In most cases, no. You will still be able to recall the incident. When the memory of a past failure comes to the surface, simply remember this: *God forgives and forgets.* Thank him for his forgiveness and intentional forgetfulness. It's settled, done. Bolt the door on haunting memories in your mental closet.

Day Four Time Out

Power Thoughts for Your Time Alone with God

*If God—the Creator of the Universe, the ultimate judge of all, the one who night and day is surrounded by angels saying, "Holy, holy, holy is the L*ORD *God Almighty"—chooses to forgive you, then who are you to doubt what God has done? Accept his forgiveness.*

❏ Read James 5:13-20.

❏ The word "confess" in James 5:16 is essentially the same as "confess" in 1 John 1:9 (both come from the same Greek word meaning "to agree with, to say one and the same thing"). The word for "confess" in James 5:16 has a prefix with it meaning "to confess out, to express verbally." James is saying, "Agree with God and another person about your sins and faults, and ask them to pray for your healing."

❏ Do you have a close friend to share your regrets with? God promises healing from "confessing our sins to one another." If you share with your small group, they must be committed to absolute confidentiality. There may be some regrets that are deeply personal, and you may not feel open to share them with the group. Instead, ask God for a mature and understanding believer to be your prayer partner. Some issues may need to be processed with a Christian counselor or pastor.

4. Agree with God regarding his future for you.

Set free from regrets, you can look to a bright future.

> *"For I know the plans I have for you," declares the LORD, "plans to prosper you and not to harm you, plans to give you hope and a future. Then you will call upon me and come and pray to me, and I will listen to you. You will seek me and find me when you seek me with all your heart."* (Jer. 29:11-13)

The prison doors to the jail cell of condemnation and regrets have flung open. Walk out, walk free. *Therefore, there is now no condemnation for those who are in Christ Jesus* (Rom. 8:1). Now run the race without being tripped up. Hebrews 12:1-2 says, *Let us strip off every weight that slows us down, especially the sin that so easily trips us up. And let us run with endurance the race God has set before us. We do this by keeping our eyes on Jesus* (NLT). Sin will entangle and trip you up, but what is the weight that slows you down? I believe the weight is self-condemnation, guilt, and shame. Strip off the weight of regrets, and run the race with God-confidence.

What can you do to safeguard your future from regrets? First, when you sin, be quick to confess your sin—agree with God—and then move forward by casting off the weight of self-condemnation. Second, do an inventory of potential "regret ruts" you tend to get into. What behaviors need to be checked or abandoned? What decisions need to be made now to prevent future regrets? Ask God for his guidance.

> *I will instruct you and teach you in the way you should go; I will counsel you and watch over you. Do not be like the horse or the mule, which have no understanding but must be controlled by bit and bridle or they will not come to you.* (Ps. 32:8-9)

Deal with stubbornness. Choose wise behavior. For example, choose to safeguard your marriage. Don't allow yourself to be alone with a member of the opposite sex in an inappropriate setting. This is a regret

THE EDGE

safeguard. As noted earlier, not all regrets are sinful behavior. Some are safety and good sense issues. Live your life making safe choices. Allow some margins in your schedule so you don't drive at break-neck speeds to get somewhere. This is a safeguard against a needless accident.

I hate losing stuff—leaving my sunglasses or my jacket somewhere because I was in a hurry or forgetful. My goal for this year: "Don't lose anything but a few extra pounds." As a discipline, I attempt to make a careful check before leaving a location. Think behaviors through in advance. Study the regrets others experience. You don't have to experience every regret yourself; you're not missing anything. Have you ever heard anyone make these statements?

- "I regret eating right and taking care of my body."
- "I regret never experimenting with illegal drugs."
- "I regret wearing a seatbelt and choosing to drive safely."
- "I regret saving myself for my marriage partner."

I have *never* heard anyone make any of these statements. Making wise choices now can prevent future "regret ruts."

When a Regret Resurfaces

You may find that even though you experience release from a regret, it may be re-triggered by a memory or something someone says. This is particularly true when someone will not forgive you and continues to bring up your failure. Also, Satan is your accuser (Rev. 12:10), and he will taunt you with your past sins and failures. Take these three steps whenever regrets return.

1. Picture yourself declared blameless in the presence of God.

Stop thinking about your regret. Rather than letting it take over your mind, *resist the devil, and he will flee from you* (James 4:7). Don't fight it; replace it. The verse for meditation this week is powerful. God has declared you blameless in his sight. Add some of the other verses mentioned in this chapter and write them on cards to carry with you. Memorize one or several to focus on when a regretful thought returns.

2. Don't get frustrated trying to forgive yourself.

This is relying on human strength. Ask yourself, *Who am I to argue with God?* Remember, forgiveness is simply agreeing with God. You can't earn forgiveness. It's God's love gift for you. Listen to God speak, and accept his forgiveness.

3. Remember you're completely forgiven and forever loved.

My mother was constantly overwhelmed with the wonder of God's extravagant grace. In a tribute to her life, I wrote this for her memorial service. Today I carry this in my personal growth notebook and refer to it often, particularly when I'm disappointed in myself.

> **Forever Loved**
> God loves me with an everlasting love, and I am forgiven and forever set free from condemnation and judgment. God through Christ has made me holy and blameless, and there is nothing I can do to improve my standing before God. As Christ was crucified and resurrected, I am crucified with him and resurrected with him, giving me power over sin and newness of life. God's amazing grace freely paid the price for my sin, granting me the gift of eternal life ... forever, forever, forever, and forever!

Leveraging Regrets

Georgia Tech and the University of California squared off for the big football game on New Year's Day, 1929, in the Rose Bowl. Prior to the end of the first half, Roy Riegels recovered a fumble for California, but then to everyone's shock, he became confused and ran in the wrong direction. Fortunately, before scoring for Georgia Tech, a teammate named Benny Lom chased him down the field and tackled him. Riegel's mistake cost his team sixty-five yards, and California was forced to kick. Georgia Tech blocked the punt and scored a safety, which proved to be the final margin of victory for Georgia Tech.

THE EDGE

In the dressing room at half-time, Riegels sat in a corner staring at the floor with a blanket around his shoulders. With his face in his hands, the big football player began to sob. Coach Price said little as he pondered the question on everyone's mind: *Should I play Riegels in the second half?* At the three-minute announcement, Coach Price said, "Men, the same team that played the first half will start the second." As the players filed out of the dressing room, Riegels remained in his corner, feeling like a failure to himself and the team. The coach came over and said, "Roy, didn't you hear me? The same team that played the first half will start the second." With his cheeks wet with tears, Roy looked up and said, "Coach, I can't do it to save my life. I've ruined you. I've ruined myself. I couldn't face that crowd in the stadium to save my life." Coach Price put a hand on his shoulder and said, "Roy, get up and go on back; the game is only half over." Riegels went back, and the Georgia Tech players would testify that no one played a tougher game of football in the second half than Roy Riegels.[43]

Regrets properly processed have the potential for strong, positive motivation. Regrets have positive potential—a hidden, camouflaged benefit. From regrets, you become aware of your own weakness, learn compassion for others who fail, and develop stronger faith. Filled with gratitude, live your remaining days running full-throttle for God. Turn the weakness of your regrets into tender compassion for others and an unwavering commitment to Christ.

David's sin was shameful, scandalous, and he was miserable carrying around his heavy load of regrets—lust, adultery, cover-up, deceit, and murder. Dragging himself through life with searing back pain, loss of health, feeling feeble and crushed with heart palpitations and failing strength, the sparkle gone from his eyes, overwhelmed with festering wounds, depressed, mourning, and groaning, David was a miserable mess.

What changed everything? David accepted God's forgiveness as *his* forgiveness. Regrets will cause you to run *from* God or run *to* God. Many believe King David wrote Psalm 71. If so, it's likely he wrote it near the end of his life. The Psalmist exclaims, *I run for dear life to* GOD, *I'll never live to regret it* (Ps. 71:1 MSG). God's evaluation of David: *I have found David son of Jesse a man after my own heart* (Acts 13:22).

What is the deep, shameful regret that rattles in the closet of your mind? Release it, and accept God's full, unconditional forgiveness.

Don't argue with God. Simply agree with his forgiveness.

David hit bottom in agonizing shame. But he didn't stay there. God flung the prison door to the jail cell of regrets wide open, and David walked out—free. He became a man after God's own heart. David's words live on, words for you in this life-changing moment—your moment to find release from the prison of regrets.

If you make a run for God—you won't regret it!
(Ps. 2:12 MSG)

Day Five Time Out

Power Thoughts for Your Time Alone with God

God loves me with an everlasting love, and I am forgiven and forever set free from condemnation and judgment.

❑ Read Psalm 51:1-19.

❑ Complete the "My Agreeing with God Agreement," which follows. You are set free. Destroy the list you made earlier.

My Agreeing with God Agreement

Dear Lord Jesus,

Let's talk about my regrets. You died on the cross to purchase the forgiveness of all my sins. You paid the price in full. I agree with you regarding my regrets. I blew it. I was wrong. I messed up. I acknowledge and confess my sin. Rather than trying to forgive myself, I will accept *your* forgiveness as *my* forgiveness.

You promised, *I will remember your sin no more* (Is. 43:25). You wipe the slate clean, you erase my regrets, you remove them as far as the east is from the west, and you bury them in the deepest sea with a sign that says, "No fishing."

Thank you that you forgive, and you forget. I completely accept and acknowledge your forgiveness. When I fail in the future, which will certainly occur, I will confess and then immediately agree with you and accept your forgiveness.

Fill me with the Holy Spirit and empower me to live my remaining days with compassion and understanding for others and a deep desire to serve you.

Thank you for your eternal forgetfulness. Right now I join David in a forgiveness celebration: *Oh, what joy for those whose disobedience is forgiven, whose sin is put out of sight! Yes, what joy for those whose record the* LORD *has cleared of guilt, whose lives are lived in complete honesty!* (Ps. 32:1-2 NLT).

_____   _____
             Signed   Date

STRENGTH TEAM

SESSION FIVE
RELEASING REGRETS

Releasing regrets is the flipside to releasing resentments, the focus of our last session. While resentments have to do with others and forgiving them, regrets have to do with ourselves and accepting God's forgiveness. If you're alive, you inevitably have regrets, things you wish you could do over in a different way. In this session, we're going to celebrate with David the Psalmist: *What happiness for those whose guilt has been forgiven! What joys when sins are covered over! What relief for those who have confessed their sins and God has cleared their record* (Ps. 32:1 TLB). Let the celebration begin!

CONNECT

❑ As a group, share how you'd complete this phrase: "If only ..."

Your response may be lighthearted: "If only I'd set the timer when I put the roast in the oven ..." or more serious: "If only I'd kept my mouth shut when ..."

GROW

❑ Read aloud as a group 2 Samuel 11:1-17.

Imagine yourselves as a reporter for *The Jerusalem Times*, and you're interviewing David toward the close of his life. What do you think his responses would be? (Or have someone role-play being David.)

Question #1: David, how did covering up your sin backfire in your life?

Question #2: How did your personal failings affect your relationship with God, your family, and other people?

THE EDGE

Question #3: How did it affect your relationship with Bathsheba when she became your wife? Did she ever use this against you?

Question #4: How did you feel after the Bathsheba affair? How was your physical, mental, and emotional health affected?

Question #5: How did you become a man after God's own heart?

APPLY

- As a group, discuss your "regret safeguards" in these areas. These may include safety and good sense decisions as well as moral and integrity issues.

    1. Health Safeguards

    2. Safety Safeguards

    3. Family Safeguards

    4. Moral and Integrity Safeguards

5. Financial Safeguards

❑ Read aloud in unison the "Changing My Mind" verse for this week.

> **Blameless**
>
> *For he chose us in him before the creation of the world to be holy and blameless in his sight.*
>
> (Eph. 1:4 NIV)
>
> 🕊 **Changing My Mind – Week 5**

PRAYER AND COMMUNION

❑ Read these verses from Psalm 51 as a group. Pause after each verse to allow for brief, silent prayer.

Have mercy on me, O God, according to your unfailing love; according to your great compassion blot out my transgressions. Wash away all my iniquity and cleanse me from my sin. (vv. 1-2)

Let me hear joy and gladness; let the bones you have crushed rejoice. Hide your face from my sins and blot out all my iniquity. Create in me a pure heart, O God, and renew a steadfast spirit within me. (vv. 8-10)

The sacrifices of God are a broken spirit; a broken and contrite heart, O God, you will not despise. (v. 17)

❑ Slowly read aloud the "My Agreeing with God Agreement" below, and then sign it.

THE EDGE

My Agreeing with God Agreement

Dear Lord Jesus,

Let's talk about my regrets. You died on the cross to purchase the forgiveness of all my sins. You paid the price in full. I agree with you regarding my regrets. I blew it. I was wrong. I messed up. I acknowledge and confess my sin. Rather than trying to forgive myself, I will accept your forgiveness as my forgiveness.

You promised, *I will remember your sin no more* (Is. 43:25). You wipe the slate clean, you erase my regrets, you remove them as far as the east is from the west, and you bury them in the deepest sea with a sign that says, "No fishing."

Thank you that you forgive, and you forget. I completely accept and acknowledge your forgiveness. When I fail in the future, which will certainly occur, I will confess and then immediately agree with you and accept your forgiveness.

Fill me with the Holy Spirit and empower me to live my remaining days with compassion and understanding for others and a deep desire to serve you.

Thank you for your eternal forgetfulness. Right now I join David in a forgiveness celebration: *Oh, what joy for those whose disobedience is forgiven, whose sin is put out of sight! Yes, what joy for those whose record the LORD has cleared of guilt, whose lives are lived in complete honesty!* (Ps. 32:1-2 NLT).

_____   _____
        Signed   Date

- ❏ Together, share communion (sometimes called "The Lord's Supper" or "The Eucharist," which means "to give thanks"). Churches often have different traditions about how communion should be served, but this is a simple procedure that works well in a small group.

Suggested Preparation and Procedure for Serving Communion in a Small Group

- ❏ Have a loaf of bread or matzo crackers along with a goblet of juice prepared and ready.

- ❏ The group leader reads 1 Corinthians 11:23-26 and leads in prayer, thanking the Lord Jesus for his broken body and shed blood, which cleanses from all sin.

- ❏ One way to serve communion is for each group member to serve another member. The leader takes the bread, tears off a portion, and holds it until the juice is passed. Turning to the person on their right, the leader says, "This represents the body of Christ broken for you." This person takes the bread, tears off a portion, and holds it until the juice is passed. They then turn to the person on their right and say, "This represents the body of Christ broken for you." Proceed around the group, with everyone holding the bread until the juice is served.

- ❏ The leader takes the goblet of juice. Turning to the person on their right, the leader says, "This represents the blood of Christ shed for you." The person takes the goblet, dips the bread in it, and eats the bread. They present the goblet to the person on their right, and say, "This represents the blood of Christ shed for you." Proceed around the group. The leader is the last to be served.

- ❏ As an alternative, the group leader may serve communion to each person.

- ❏ Close by singing "Amazing Grace" or another appropriate song.

- ❏ As a group, discuss doing a deed of kindness or giving a love gift for a needy person or family this week.

THE EDGE
SHARE

☐ How do you open the door to share your faith? Learn the fine art of asking a thought-provoking question. Look for the opportunity to get a conversation started this week using these questions:

  • *Is it possible to live regret free?*

  • *What hope is there for a person who's unable to forgive themselves?*

☐ Be prepared to share one of your regrets and how you've been set free.

CHAPTER SIX

WHY CAN'T YOU BE MORE LIKE ME?

Differences are the sandpaper God uses to polish the rough edges of our character.

Whether it's a relationship with a friend, co-worker, college roommate, or family member, differences can be a major source of frustration. If you're in the same household with an opposite, how do you maintain sanity when differences grate and irritate? This is the jagged edginess of relationships. Does it work to try to change someone? Is it possible? Is there a way to cooperate with God as he works to change someone? Let's look at some principles to be an agent for change—whether work, school, sports, church, or small group. Strengths and weaknesses play a big part in the success or failure of a relationship.

Compatibility

It's a good idea to identify some degree of compatibility before selecting a college roommate or a friend to rent an apartment with you. Colleges and universities now attempt to match dorm roommates based on sleep and study habits, room temperature, likes and dislikes. With the increase in divorce due to irreconcilable differences, perhaps applicants for a marriage license should complete a "compatibility quiz." A simple test could be devised to check for agreeable temperament in such matters as noise tolerance level, messiness or tidiness, nocturnal tendencies, eating habits, mean room temperature ... and general meanness. Here's my quiz to kick things off.

Compatibility Quiz
(Check those that apply)

1. ___Snores at night; ___Complains about those who snore; ___Talks in sleep; ___Walks in sleep; ___Wheezes in sleep
2. ___Answers phone immediately; ___Unplugs the phone; ___Yells for others to answer the phone
3. ___Reads in bed; ___Clips fingernails in bed; ___Sleeps in bed; ___Eats in bed; ___Hoards covers in bed; ___Flosses teeth in bed
4. ___Doesn't like pets; ___Likes some pets; ___Feeds the dog at the table; ___Bathes with the dog; ___Doesn't bathe with the dog, but bathes less frequently than the dog
5. ___Wants things neat and clean; ___Tidy, but not super neat; ___Three years behind on spring cleaning; ___Thinks dust is decorative
6. ___Listens to elevator music; ___Likes country music; ___Likes anything with lots of volume; ___Addicted to silence; ___Thinks earbuds are jewelry; ___Listens to stereo, watches TV, reads newspaper while listening to spouse
7. Interval for bathroom stops on vacation: ___10 minutes; ___30 minutes; ___2 hours; ___4 hours; ___2 days
8. Electric blanket setting: ___1; ___4; ___7; ___10 with 3 quilts, thermostat on 78
9. ___Eager to get up before the sun gets up; ___Eager to get up before the sun sets
10. Arrival time for events: ___5 to 15 minutes early; ___30 seconds early; ___5 to 15 minutes late; ___Thinks departure and arrival times are the same; ___Enjoys being late to make a "grand entrance"[44]

While this is intended for fun, it strikes a serious note. The issues underlying compatibility are serious stuff. Bottom line: *God designed people with vastly different likes and dislikes.* For example, it's normal for brothers and sisters—raised in the same household with the same parents, the same value system and training—to have uniquely different personalities and temperaments, respond differently to the training, and go different directions in life.

Nationally recognized personal development speaker and writer Earl Nightingale shared this research in an article titled "How to React to Stress."

> Two young boys were raised by an alcoholic father. As they grew older, they moved away from that broken home, each going his own way in the world. Several years later, they happened to be interviewed separately by a psychologist who was analyzing the effects of drunkenness on children in broken homes. His research revealed that the two men were strikingly different from each other. One was a clean-living teetotaler; the other, a hopeless drunk like his father. The psychologist asked each of them why he developed the way he did, and each gave an identical answer, "What else would you expect when you have a father like mine?"[45]

If you're a parent with more than one child, are your children different from each other? I'm sure you've discovered differences in their temperaments. Are they similar to you or quite different? Just when moms and dads think they're getting the first child figured out, along comes the second one. And they find themselves thinking, *Where did this one come from? This one must be* your *child. He or she is a total opposite of me.*

Personally, I think God should have started us out with grandchildren. You know, have them over for the weekend and see how it goes. On Sunday afternoon, pack their stuff up and send them back to their parents who are highly qualified because they received their five-year grandparent apprentice training before becoming "real parents." This would allow potential moms and dads to sharpen some parenting skills and develop a clear-cut game plan before having children of their own. Instead, God gives inexperienced, naïve parents a predesigned little bundle of mischief stamped "no refund, no return," and says, "See if you can figure this one out."

God could have designed everyone perfectly compatible—sleeping and waking up at the same time, liking the same foods, enjoying the same music, amused by the same jokes, fancying the same colors. How boring!

God, the Creator, is creative. He designs each person with meticulous detail; no two people have the same fingerprint or DNA. Differences are God's signature indicating, "You're one of a kind; you're special." Why, other than being infinitely creative, did God design people differently? Differences are the sandpaper God uses to polish the rough edges of our character.

Day One Time Out

Power Thoughts for Your Time Alone with God

Differences are God's signature saying, "You're one of a kind—you're special."

- ❏ Read Romans 12:6-16. Identify and underline key phrases in this passage for loving, understanding, and appreciating others.

- ❏ Chart your profile of strengths and weaknesses, along with those of your spouse or close friend.

Your Profile

Strengths	Weaknesses

Their Profile

Strengths	Weaknesses

- ❏ How did God design you differently than the person you're closest to? In what ways are your talents, gifts, and skills different? What do you appreciate about that person? Have you told them so?

- ❏ Go to the back of your book and cut out or copy the meditation verse for this week titled "Accept One Another." Put it on your bathroom mirror to focus on when you're getting ready for the day and before you go to bed at night. Meditate on it throughout the day as you commit it to memory.

Dave and Joanne Beckwith

Mixing and Matching

The closeness of a family relationship best illustrates differences that can cause friction. These principles are at play in virtually all relationships.

Jerry and Alice had been married for nineteen years and needed few reminders that they were opposites. Jerry was a high-energy, athletic, outgoing, optimistic forty-six-year-old. Early to bed, early to rise, he could outwork and outrun most men half his age or half-again his size. Highly disciplined and meticulous about what he ate, he scolded others for eating "junk foods." His wife, Alice, was quiet, reserved, and cautious, with a melancholy sweetness. Meeting people was difficult and awkward for Alice, but those who took the time to get to know her discovered a kind, resourceful, and refreshing person. Alice was sensitive, caring, and compassionate. She'd nurse a wounded stray kitten for weeks or work until two a.m. to put together the costume for her daughter's school play. Jerry was fun to meet, with his quick wit and bubbly personality. Alice made friends slowly but developed intense loyalty. She was sluggish through most of the day but came alive about eight p.m.—just when Jerry was winding down. Their individual profiles can be summarized like this:

Profile of Jerry
Age 46

Strengths	Weaknesses
1. Skilled talker, communicator	1. Impatient listener
2. Outgoing, friendly	2. Sometimes superficial
3. Persistent, determined	3. Conniving
4. Disciplined	4. Rigid, critical
5. Courageous	5. Reckless, impulsive
6. Skilled, thorough	6. Picky, demanding

THE EDGE

Profile of Alice
Age 41

Strengths	Weaknesses
1. Excellent listener	1. Quiet, withdrawn
2. Compassionate	2. Overly sentimental
3. Perceptive about people	3. People-pleaser
4. Sensitive	4. Easily hurt
5. Accepting of others	5. Lenient
6. Loyal, dedicated	6. Possessive

When looking at Jerry and Alice's strengths and weaknesses, you'll notice two things: 1) strengths often have a weak side; and 2) opposites often attract. Years earlier, during their courtship, Jerry and Alice fell in love with the person whose strengths complemented their weaknesses. Within a short time, appreciation for the strengths of their mate was replaced by irritation with their weaknesses. As a result, the unappreciated strengths diminished. "Why can't you be more like me?" was more than an occasional comment; it was acted out in the frustration of every day. A struggle began as each attempted to change the other.

To complicate matters further, they had two children, fifteen-year-old Shawna, and eleven-year-old Taylor. Shawna quiet the free spirit with an outgoing, friendly personality. She made friends easily and loved to hang out with them. Life was a lark, and she was the free-flying bird. She was critical of her dad's perfectionism and became infuriated when he said, "If you'd develop some discipline in your life, you could amount to something."

Taylor was a different combo. With technical skills, he loved tinkering with a computer, phone, or game. He could surf the Internet for hours while life floated by. Taylor grew sullen when Dad said, "Taylor, why don't you make friends like Shawna does? If you were friendlier, you'd have lots of friends." Shawna's school grades were below average (and well below her ability) while Taylor's grades were excellent.

Jerry and Alice's lack of appreciation for each other translated into sharp differences over how to raise Shawna and Taylor. Jerry rode Shawna and Taylor to shape up while Alice did the opposite. Alice's leniency with Shawna and Taylor irritated Jerry. He felt undermined when she said, within earshot of both kids, "Jerry, just lighten up on Shawna and Taylor. You're always coming down on them." Life became a daily battle—attempting to change one another and refusing to change themselves.

Pressure and Resistance to Change

Stated as a general principle that Murphy (of the infamous "Murphy's Law") would approve: *the more you attempt to change someone, the more they resist change.* The pressure to change produces an equal or greater resistance to change. The greater the driving forces to change, the greater the resistance to change.

Picture this scene: a husband drops his clothes on the floor each night to the aggravation of his meticulous wife. Watch the driving and resistance forces in this exchange.

> *Wife:* "Would you please hang up your clothes so I don't have to walk over them or iron them again?"
> *Husband:* "Whatever." (He's heard this before.)
>
> [Nothing changes. He continues to drop his clothes on the floor.]
>
> *Wife:* "Honey, I told you to pick up your clothes so I don't have to pick them up. I'm not your mother, you know."
> *Husband:* "They're my clothes, so don't get uptight. I earned the money to buy them, and it doesn't hurt if they're on the floor."
> *Wife:* "They may be your clothes, but I have to wash and iron them."
> *Husband:* "Fine. Don't wash and iron them. I'll take them to the cleaners."
>
> *Wife:* "Take them to the cleaners? We can't afford that!"
>
> *Husband:* "Well, with the way my shirt looked after you ironed it last time, I should have left it on the floor."

Wife: "What? If I didn't spend all my time picking up after you, I'd have more time to do a careful job of ironing."

[Since words are not succeeding, she devises a clever plan: she hides clothes left on the floor. One morning, he notices his closet is depleted.]

Husband: "Where did all my slacks and shirts go? I'm missing socks too."

Wife: "Well, have you been picking them up? When I was growing up if I didn't pick up my clothes, my mother put them away until I learned to pick them up."

Husband: "I didn't marry your mother. Don't you ever pull that again. I'll leave my clothes any place I like."

And I repeat: The greater the pressure to change, the greater the resistance to change. The result? A stubborn standoff, with hostility in the relationship. The Scripture says, *A tenderhearted person lives a blessed life; a hardhearted person lives a hard life* (Prov. 28:14 MSG). Or to put it another way, *the stubborn are headed for serious trouble* (Prov. 28:14 NLT). "Hardheadedness" makes for "hardheartedness," which makes for a "hard life." The affection that was once in the relationship has turned sour; the love cord is kinked. The pressure to change simmers under the surface, with occasional explosions. Home becomes an emotional, toxic dumpsite, brimming with anger and resentment. Without a resolution, separation or divorce may seem to be the only solution.

This illustration applies in marriage, but also in cooperative efforts at many levels—friendships, sports teams, work partnerships. Put this book down for a minute and align the tips of your fingers and thumb on your left hand with the tips of the fingers and thumb on your right hand. Push them hard against each other. Can your right hand over-power your left hand or vice versa? Maybe, but generally the force of one equals the resistance of the other. Now, release the pressure and allow your left and right fingers and thumbs to slide past each other forming a clasped hand, a oneness of left and right hand. This strong bond illustrates oneness.

The fingers and thumbs on your left and right hand are what I call "identical opposites." They're uniquely different—virtual opposites—but uniquely similar and clearly designed for each other. There are many things you can't do without using both hands. They're intended to work together though often performing opposite functions. Try opening a jar, driving a nail, or buttoning your shirt with one hand—rather difficult. I've often met with two people in a standoff, pressuring the other to change, somewhat like the right hand saying to the left hand, "When will you figure it out? You're designed backwards. Why don't you change and get it right, like me?"

What is the solution? Stop trying to fix each other. When the pressure to change is removed, the resistance to change begins to diminish. Ask forgiveness for nagging, pressuring, manipulating, resisting, pouting, etc. Begin to accept one another—after all, God designed each of us with unique differences and complementary gifts. When this happens, the bond in the relationship becomes like the two hands, tightly connected but also working harmoniously to perform what couldn't be done separately. When husband and wife accept their God-designed differences and accept one another as their "identical opposite," their differences become essential components in their oneness.

Day Two Time Out

Power Thoughts for Your Time Alone with God

The pressure to change produces an equal or greater resistance to change.

❏ How have you seen the above statement to be true in your relationships?

❏ Read James 3:13-18. What are the characteristics of the world's wisdom and God's wisdom? Write these in two columns to compare them.

World's Wisdom	God's Wisdom

❏ Identify steps you can take today to apply God's wisdom in your life.

How God Changes People

It seems that when I try to change someone, it backfires. Is there a better way? What brings about change? Do I have a part in the process? Here are key principles to get a firm grip on.

1. God changes people, and I'm not God.

God changes people on his schedule, not mine. God changes people in his way, not mine. My role is to surrender the process to God and allow him to do his work in his time. Ecclesiastes 3:11 says, *God has made everything beautiful in its own time.* God coordinates the process and the schedule.

Stop thinking, *I'll get them straightened out if you help me, Lord.* Instead, surrender the process to God. From personal experience, when I've attempted to change someone, the results have been at best disappointing and at worst disastrous. They may change for a short time to get me off their back, only to revert to their old behavior. In the end, they resent me for playing God in their life.

If you're under the assumption that it's your responsibility to change someone, I have disconcerting news for you: you're setting yourself up for disappointment. Surrender to God any tendency to manipulate, nag, control, or use gimmicks. The resentment produced by these human tactics usually boomerangs. Take the "I'm out to change you" badge off your shirt.

2. Know your responsibility—where it begins and where it ends.

If you're a parent, employer, or supervisor, you have an important role to correct and discipline when needed. Even with this responsibility, it's still God who does the changing. When the relationship is a friend, spouse, co-worker, team member, etc., you have a responsibility to speak the truth in love and exhort at the appropriate time. This isn't an excuse to be passive; it simply recognizes that God is the CEO of the "change department."

Where do I begin? What is top priority? Begin with yourself; be open regarding your weaknesses, and be active in identifying your weaknesses and allowing God to turn them into strengths. You can

THE EDGE

really take responsibility for just one person, and that's you. My hunch is that, if you're at all like me, you have your hands full taking care of your own weaknesses.

3. Choose to cooperate with God, using the ABC's.

Here are the big three: **A**ccept them with unconditional love; **B**elieve in God's power and their potential; **C**ommunicate the truth in love. These three steps allow God to work the process of transformation in someone's life, and they also allow you to be a participant, being used by God but without manipulating or nagging. Throughout each step, pray, pray, and pray some more. In particular, pray for yourself. Pray you'll stay surrendered. Pray you'll not grow impatient. Pray you won't mess things up. Ask God to give you grace.

Accept
Them with Unconditional Love
Love hopes all things.
(1 Cor. 13:7)

What's the meaning of love? Love is a dangerously misused word; we use it for all kinds of things. We love ice cream, we love our dog or cat, we love a singer we've never met, we love our car or stereo system, and we use the same word to express the lifetime commitment to the one we care about more than anyone else in the world. If you look up love in the twenty-two-volume print edition of *World Book Encyclopedia*, you won't find even one article on love. It simply says, "See sex, emotions."

Speaking to a class at a public school on "How to Tell if You're in Love," I asked this question: "Is love a noun or a verb?" A wise-cracking guy piped up, "I think love is a noun most of the time, but on Friday and Saturday night it's a verb." We think of love as something that happens on some enchanted evening across a crowded room. Is the love still there on some exhausted evening when the two-year-old is sick for the third time this month, you've been laid off from your job, the electricity is about to be turned off, the washing machine quit, and the stack of unpaid bills seems higher than your wedding cake? You can feel the edginess in the air and in the words that are spoken. It will take more than euphoric feelings from some enchanted evening to make it through some exhausted evening.

What does it mean when someone says, "I love you"? Girls (and guys too) are often swept off their feet when they hear these words. Before falling off the love cliff, I recommend asking for clarification: "Thank you. I deeply appreciate your expression of love. To help me understand, what type of love are you referring to, Type A, B, F, or S?" The Greeks wisely distinguished different types of love by using four different words.

Type B: Biological Love

Key question: *"When you say you love me, do you mean the type of love you have for your sister or your grandma?"*

The Greeks used the word *storge* or *stergein* to describe this love. This is family love, the natural love of parents for their children, children for their parents, grandparents for their grandchildren, love of a husband and wife since they are one flesh, and a healthy and appropriate love between brothers and sisters. This is a love that's based in one's own nature, biologically rooted from shared genetics. It's non-sexual. A parent may be steaming mad with their child, and five minutes later feel overwhelming compassion and love for that same child. Brothers and sisters may fight incessantly, yet be ready to defend their sibling against anyone who'd attack them. Fighting adolescent siblings often become the deepest of friends as adults. This word stergein is used in a negative sense meaning *unloving* or *without natural affection* in Romans 1:31 and 2 Timothy 3:3.

Type F: Friendship Love

Key question: *"When you say you love me, do you mean you like me as a friend, a buddy, someone you enjoy hanging out with?"*

The Greeks used the word *philein* or *philos* to describe shared friendship between two people. The word in its various forms is used forty-five times in the New Testament. Philadelphia (which means "city of brotherly love") derives its name from this word. Friendship love is rooted in a pleasurable glow of the heart, kindled by genuine affection, fondness, and liking.[46] Whether it's a person or an object, it's pleasure-

THE EDGE

producing. In a non-relational sense, when you say, "I love my car" or "I love ice cream," this is "Type F" love—the object produces a warm glow of liking. When the object no longer gives you a pleasurable feeling, the love of liking ends.

In a relationship, philos is a "you like me" and "I like you" pleasurable attraction. Yes, there are fair-weather friendships, but don't underestimate the power of non-erotic devoted friendships that run deep and weather many storms. As Proverbs says, *A friend loves at all times, and a brother is born for adversity* (17:17), and *Wounds from a friend can be trusted, but an enemy multiplies kisses* (27:6).

Friendship love may be accompanied by appropriate physical touch—the "holy kiss" (*philema*) was a non-erotic gesture of Christian love. As a believer, it's natural to have a love for your brothers and sisters in Christ—you're born again into the same family. Romans 12:10 combines Type B Biological Love with Type F Friendship Love.

> *Be devoted* [Greek word *philostorgos*, combined word of friendship love and biological love] *to one another in brotherly love* [Greek word *philadelphias*, friendship love]; *give preference to one another in honor.* (Rom. 12:10, definitions supplied)

The true-life story of Gayle Sayers and Brian Piccolo, featured in the outstanding movie *Brian's Song*, is a classic on friendship that moved me to tears.

> Gayle Sayers and Brian Piccolo, star running backs for the Chicago Bears, created a sensation as the first black and white men in professional football to room together. Reporters asked them about it. Reporter: "Do you mind living with him?" Piccolo: "Not if he doesn't use the bathroom." Reporter: "What do you two fellows talk about?" Sayers: "Oh, just the usual racist talk." They kidded each other a lot, but there was deep affection between them.
> Then Piccolo contracted cancer and began to spend more time in the hospital than on the football field. The two had planned to go with their wives to the Professional

Football Writers Association banquet in New York, where Sayers was to be presented the George S. Halas Award as that year's most courageous player. But the advance of the disease rendered Piccolo unable to go.

When the moment came for Sayers to receive the award, he stepped to the microphone and with tears rolling down his cheeks, unashamedly said, "You flatter me by giving me this award. But I accept it for Brian Piccolo. Brian is the man who should receive the award. I love Brian, and I'd like you to love him, too."[47]

Type S: Sexual Love

Key question: *"When you say you love me, do you mean you find me sexually attractive, I turn you on, and you'd like to make love to me?"*

This is erotic passion, exhilarating excitement, on-fire emotions. By God's design, sexual love is "satisfaction seeking." The Greeks used the word *eros* to describe sexual love. We get our word "erotic" from it. Eros is not intrinsically evil. Erotic love is a marvelous gift from God, but it can be twisted and perverted. Sexual passion is a selfish, empty act without the other types of love.

Sexual love is *passion-based*; biological love is *parent-based*; friendship love is *pleasure-based*; and the next type of love, agape love, is *prizing-based*.

Type A: Agape Love

Key question: *"When you say you love me, are you saying you value me as a person, you accept me with my faults and flaws, you want the very best for me in every situation, and you love me so deeply, you'll wait to physically consummate our love until we're married?"*

While I direct this question to relational attraction between a male and female, agape love also applies to non-sexual relationships. This is the highest expression of love, the pinnacle, the summit. The Greeks used the word agapao in describing this type of love. This is the most frequent word for love in the New Testament, appearing over 300 times in its various forms. This is highly unusual because the Greek poets and philosophers rarely used the word agape. What is agape love?

THE EDGE

1. Agape is God.

John used three words to define agape: *God is love* (1 John 4:16), or *God is agape*. The reverse is true as well: Agape is God. He is the source, the giver of love. Agape is sacrificial love, total giving, love that knows no end. Christ displayed this love on the cross in his voluntary death for sin. *Love each other as I have loved you. Greater love has no one than this, that he lay down his life for his friends* (John 15:12-13).

2. Agape is a love of prizing.

Friendship love is based on a pleasurable, reciprocal relationship between two people; agape love is based on prizing or valuing someone. Agape "speaks of a love which is awakened by a sense of value in an object which causes one to prize it." [48] God offers this love to us, even when we're unlovable. He's in the salvaging business. He loves the discarded, the shamed, the bruised, the hurting. When friendship has long been discarded due to violations in the relationships, agape reaches out, placing value on the unlovable. *God is so rich in mercy, and he loved us so much, that even though we were dead because of our sins, he gave us life when he raised Christ from the dead. (It is only by God's grace that you have been saved!)* (Eph. 2:4-5 NLT).

3. Agape is unconditional love.

What does this mean? It means I love you ... no matter what. Unconditional love removes the "ifs." It is not agape love when you say, "I love you if you don't disappoint me. I love you *if* you change your behavior. I love you *if* you don't hurt me. I love you *if* I continue to have feelings for you." Agape or unconditional love includes these characteristics.

- Agape love doesn't condone sin.
- Agape love isn't the "silent treatment," an unspoken critical attitude.
- Agape love is the power of Christ, accepting the other person as Christ accepted you.
- Agape love is a choice, not a feeling.
- Agape love places a high value on the person.

- Agape love sees the positive potential in a glaring flaw.
- Agape love accepts the total person—strengths *and* weaknesses.
- Agape love is God's method to change a life.

4. Agape love seeks the ultimate best for the person.

Sometimes the very best for the one you love is painful and extremely difficult. Agape love doesn't mean the other person has the right to walk all over you. Agape love doesn't accept sin as inconsequential. If your business partner is stealing funds from your company; if your adult child is doing drugs and stealing money; if someone is spreading lies about you, agape love confronts the wrong. If a spouse is having an affair and refuses to end the relationship, is the wounded spouse supposed to say, "Well, that's okay. Maybe someday you'll give up that other person because I love you so much"? No!

Recently a husband came to see me. He acknowledged having an affair. I asked his wife to join us for subsequent sessions, where it became apparent the husband didn't really want help ending the relationship with the other woman. He was more interested in having me say it was acceptable and his wife should get used to it. I explained that, before God, there was no justification for his affair, and there were severe consequences for continuing. I insisted that if he was serious about doing what God required of him, he'd change his cell phone number immediately and end the relationship. I explained the consequences that would live on for years to come when their children discovered the sad news. He had to make a choice, since marriage requires being mutually exclusive for each other. In our final session, weeping and sobbing, his wife shared her heart with him: "I love you and care very deeply for you. Even if you continue in your relationship with her, my concern for you will live on. However, we're married, and you *must* make a choice between her and me. I ache for you over the consequences you'll bring on yourself, on our children, and on your long-term peace of mind and relationship with God. Please know I love you, and this is one of the hardest things I've ever done." Sadly, he left to go with the other woman. His wife didn't stop praying for him, but she also took steps to move on with her life. This is the tough side of agape love. *Love is as strong as death. ... It burns like blazing fire, like a mighty flame. Many waters cannot quench love; rivers cannot wash it away ...* (Song of Sol.

8:6-7). Love endures, even when trampled on, long after feelings have vanished.

I wish it were otherwise, but there are no guarantees that someone will change. God allows human beings to make their own choices. Some people resist God, and though God could force them to change, he chooses not to. God says, *I am letting them go their blind and stubborn way, living according to their own desires* (Ps. 81:12 TLB). Jeremiah, the weeping prophet, said, *If you still refuse to listen, I will weep alone because of your pride. My eyes will overflow with tears ...* (Jer. 13:17 NLT). When your heart is broken for someone, know God weeps with you.

5. Agape love accepts the person, strengths and weaknesses, faults and flaws.

Last summer, I led a group of men in a study and discussion on what it means to love your wife. We memorized one verse: *Love your wives* (Eph. 5:25). Then week after week, we unwrapped what this verse means. Ask some men if they love their wives, and they say, "Sure. We made love two weeks ago." Loving your wife is so much more. It's a matter of laying your life down for her deepest needs. It's self-sacrifice. Love may be doing your dishes rather than leaving them in the sink, picking up your pile of stuff that makes her so upset. I'm convinced if a careful search of police records were completed, it would show no husband has ever been shot while mopping the kitchen floor.

6. Agape love displays the character of God.

Dana Curry and Heather Mercer were held captive by the Taliban in Afghanistan. When released, they were asked, "What was the most difficult thing in your Afghan experience?" They said, "It was learning to live with six women in a very small room. We had to learn to forgive each other a lot." Forgiveness is among the identifiable characteristics of agape love in 1 Corinthians 13.

> 1. *Love is patient* with the faults of others (accepting them and trusting God to bring about change in his time).
>
> 2. *Love is kind* (gracious, thoughtful, and sensitive to

build up rather than tear down).

3. *Love is not envious* (undercutting, spiteful, jealous).

4. *Love is not boastful* (self-centered, pushy to get its own way).

5. *Love is not proud* (not displaying an independent, stubborn spirit, resisting advice, refusing to acknowledge wrongs and ask forgiveness).

6. *Love is not rude* (not insensitive, irritable, touchy, making a scene).

7. *Love is not self-seeking* (instead, it is flexible, gentle, easy to work with, not demanding its own way).

8. *Love is not easily angered* (popping off, easily provoked, hot-headed).

9. *Love keeps no record of wrongs* (doesn't hold a grudge or bring up the past, but chooses to forgive).

10. *Love does not delight in evil* (divisive, spreading gossip, taking revenge, practicing deceit), *but rejoices with the truth.*

11. *Love always protects the reputation* of others (seeking to give a good report, remaining loyal, and guarding confidential information).

12. *Love always trusts* (believing what God can do).

13. *Love always hopes* (anticipating what God will do).

14. *Love always perseveres* (enduring despite hardships and misunderstandings).

15. *Love never fails* (never giving up or falling away).

Great friendships are rich with agape love and commitment. There's no finer example of agape love in friendship than the relationship between David and Jonathan.

THE EDGE

After David had finished talking with Saul, Jonathan became one in spirit with David, and he loved him as himself. ... And Jonathan made a covenant with David because he loved him as himself. Jonathan took off the robe he was wearing and gave it to David, along with his tunic, and even his sword, his bow and his belt. (1 Sam. 18:1, 3-4)

Jonathan's commitment to David is astounding since David stood in the way of Jonathan's right to become king. Jonathan's entire career was in jeopardy due to his commitment to support David. Note: absolutely nothing indicates there was a sexual relationship between these two men. Those who try to read this into the account twist and distort the Scripture.

Four-dimensional love

Since God intended sexual love exclusively for the marital union of a man and a woman, marriage alone offers four-dimensional love. In a Spirit-filled marriage, agape love includes the other three types of love: sexual, biological, and friendship. Biological love is the bond of oneness (*bone of my bones, flesh of my flesh,* Gen. 2:23), friendship love is the pleasure of companionship, sexual love is the intimacy of passion, and agape love is valuing each other as a priceless treasure. Four-dimensional love is God's ultimate for a human relationship.

Day Three Time Out

Power Thoughts for Your Time Alone with God

Agape love accepts the total person, strengths and weaknesses.

❑ What is the most difficult relationship you have faced in applying the quote above?

❑ Read Romans 15:1-7, 13.

❑ In what ways did Christ accept you as a person? If you accept the person you identified in the opening question, what will this mean in practical ways as you accept them as Christ accepted you? Write down specific ways to do this.

Believe
In What God Will Do
Love believes all things.
(1 Cor. 13:7)

How often have you heard someone say, "Just believe in yourself"? I tried believing in myself. What a mess and disappointment! Proverbs 28:26 says bluntly, *He who trusts in himself is a fool.* God never tells you to believe in yourself.

You may have heard someone with a track record of failure say, "No one believes in me. How can I believe in myself when no one else supports me? Will you believe in me?" I hear their heart cry, but rather than setting them up for more failure, I respond, "God has a better plan for you than believing in yourself or having others believe in you. That's a formula for failure. I do believe in your incredible God-surrendered potential. Let's ask him to take over." And in your own self-talk, don't put your trust in yourself. Instead, remind yourself, *I believe in what God will do with my potential as I am surrendered to him.*

The love chapter, 1 Corinthians 13, says, *Love believes all things.* What does this mean? "Believing all things" is not swallowing someone's lies and deceit, or ignoring their self-destructive lifestyle, or overlooking how others are being hurt and destroyed. "Believing all things" doesn't expect them to change themselves. "Believing all things" is faith and trust in God, with anticipation for what he will do. Where to begin?

1. Be a friend.

In turning weaknesses into strengths, the friendship role is the best. *A friend loves at all times, and a brother is born for adversity* (Prov. 17:17). Friends are those you can talk things over with and who will listen to you. They like you no matter what. They're willing to hear you out without always trying to fix you or fix the problem. They accept you. Friendship is a relationship built on trust and confidence. Henry David Thoreau said, "The most I can do for my friend is simply be his friend." In a friendship, a difficult confrontation can be weathered, knowing your friend loves you and is committed to your well-being: *Wounds from a friend can be trusted, but an enemy multiplies kisses* (Prov. 27:6).

THE EDGE

2. Appreciate their worth and value.

The word "appreciate" means to "be thankful for, to express and recognize the worth and value of someone or something." If your home appreciates, the value goes up; if your car depreciates, the value goes down. The value of an appreciated person goes up; the value of a depreciated person goes down. The Scripture is clear: ... *encourage one another daily, as long as it is called "Today," so that none of you may be hardened by sin's deceitfulness* (Heb. 3:13). Did you spot the "frequency factor" for giving encouragement? Once a year on Thanksgiving? On their birthday? Once a month, once a week? No. *Daily*! The heart of a discouraged person begins to harden, and sin dances at the door. With a simple word of encouragement, you can have an enormous impact, helping the discouraged person conquer temptation and live victoriously. Who are you going to encourage today?

Let's assume your wife or mother enjoys cooking and spends hours putting her special touch on every meal with the family—elaborate garnishes, sauces, multiple courses, specialty desserts. She could be a contestant on the cooking channel. Year after year, the family sits down and prays, "Dear Lord, we thank you for this wonderful meal. Amen." The family eats without a comment about the food. Just silence, year after year after year. What's wrong with this picture? It's good they thank God for the food, but how about thanking Mom? The family never says the food is terrible. They just say nothing—stone silence. Why? Maybe they think, *If we tell Mom she's a great cook, she'll become proud.* Nonsense! *Better is open rebuke than hidden love* (Prov. 27:5).

What eventually happens? Mom concludes that cooking really doesn't matter since no one appreciates it. She digs the leftovers out of the refrigerator, plops them on a plate, and microwaves them. Leftovers are served so often, the family wonders if she's borrowing them from the neighbors. When she doesn't want to cook, she hollers, "There's a TV dinner in the freezer. *Bon appétit.*" What? It's more like "gone appetite." What you fail to appreciate will diminish and disappear.

Write down genuine affirmation you can give to those closest to you. Now look for the right time and setting to communicate your words. When the person you're speaking to recovers from the shock, repeat it. I'm not suggesting this be done in a mechanical way or insincere manner. For your grown and married children, you may want to write an affirming letter, something like this:

> Bill, we appreciate you as a son-in-law. You came into the life of our daughter with tenderness, caring, and spiritual leadership. We know this was God's doing. Thank you for being a fine husband, father, businessman, provider, and a man of God.
>
> Susie, you're our daughter and always will be. You're such a beauty, a gem, a treasure, and we're thrilled to be Dad and Mom to you. So often you encourage us with your thoughtful words. You're a great wife, mother, and second-grade teacher. You're a person of spiritual maturity and love. We're exceptionally proud of you.
>
> Bill and Susie, we bless you both and treasure you, and pray God's greatest blessing on your home and your lives. All we can say is, "We love you both!"

Don't stick a jab in your note of affirmation: "Bill and Susie, we hope and pray you'll start having family devotions," or "We hope you get your car loan paid off soon." This will negate the entire affirmation.

Nicknames may also be used to affirm, but choose carefully since nicknames may be derogatory as well as complimentary. When you give someone a nickname, make certain it's a name they're comfortable with. Calling a son "Tiger" or a daughter "Princess" can affirm them as a person and affect how they see themselves. I gave Joanne's parents, Henry and Elizabeth, royalty nicknames: "King Henry and Queen Elizabeth." This caught on with some of the family, and it was fun to see them light up when we called them King or Queen.

3. Identify their potential.

Let's return to the home of Jerry, Alice, Shawna, and Taylor, where criticism has been thick in the air. What can be done to break through the ill feelings they have for each other? Here's a starting point:

THE EDGE

Jerry to his wife: "Alice, I'm sorry for trying to change you. You're God's special person, uniquely designed to be who you are. You're great with people, so sensitive and accepting. I admire how you make people feel loved and accepted. Thanks for being such a great listener."

Alice to her husband: "Jerry, it makes me blush when you say this, but it also makes me feel valued and appreciated. Thank you. When something needs to get done and done right, you're the man. Thanks for your hard work in providing for the family. I admire and respect you for not quitting when things get tough."

The husband needs respect and affirmation; the wife needs approval and love. If they fail in supporting one another with these positives, they'll drag each other down with their negatives, as columnist Janie B. Cheaney observed in *WORLD* magazine:

> If men and women don't mutually pledge their strengths, they will default to their weaknesses. The harder a woman pushes, the faster a man retreats. The more a man forfeits, the more a woman takes on. He gets lazy, she gets bitter. He turns violent, she becomes passive.[49]

Jerry and Alice also have the opportunity to extend this attitude to Shawna and Taylor, affirming their worth and identifying potential.

Jerry to his daughter: "Shawna, you're great with people, with your warm smile, bubbly personality, and ability to communicate. Have you ever thought about going into public relations? Some company will be thrilled to hire you. You might even make a great television news reporter. Whatever, you will do well as you follow God in your life. I'm so proud of you."

Alice to her son: "Taylor, you're so great with computers. I'm just lost with these technical things, and you're an absolute genius. I'm so blessed to have a son like you. Who knows? You may be designing the computer chip for the next trip to outer space someday."

No matter how buried or camouflaged, every person has undeveloped potential. You're in a unique position to help others by identifying their potential. What do you see in their life that they're not aware of but need encouragement in developing? Study the person, asking God in prayer, "Lord, what is _____'s undeveloped potential, and how can I encourage them in it?" In identifying potential, you're not determining God's will for their life; you're simply helping them become aware of possibilities.

Years ago I was emotionally locked up and carrying unresolved issues, but Joanne saw in me what I didn't see. I remember her saying, "You have a remarkable caring and kindness that I don't think you realize." I was surprised by her words, and she wasn't conning me. She saw in me what I didn't see and today that's who I am. Be a person who believes and anticipates what God will do.

What about telling someone you're proud of them? Many Christians are uncomfortable using the word "proud" as a word of affirmation. Being prideful is sin, and many of the biblical uses of the word "pride" do refer to sin. However, the same Greek word is used to describe bad as well as good pride. For example, Paul writes to the Corinthians, *I have great confidence in you; I take great pride in you* (2 Cor. 7:4), and again he says, *Therefore show these men the proof of your love and the reason for our pride in you, so that the churches can see it* (2 Cor. 8:24). In the book of Galatians, Paul writes, *Each one should test his own actions. Then he can take pride in himself, without comparing himself to somebody else* (Gal. 6:4). As Joseph Thayer[50] suggests, the pride condemned in the Bible is "an insolent and empty assurance which trusts in its own power and resources and shamefully despises and violates divine laws and human laws." On the other hand, when pride is approved in the Bible, it is giving glory to God for what he is doing in a person's life. They are commended for being a surrendered vessel allowing God to work. For example, one couple, both of whom were relatively new Christians, were going through a terrible time of suffering. I said to them, "I am proud of you both for standing strong in your faith." In this sense, it is appropriate to say, "I'm proud of you."

Day Four Time Out

Power Thoughts for Your Time Alone with God

The value of an appreciated person goes up.

❏ When you receive an appreciative comment from someone, what impact does that have on you, immediately and in future actions?

❏ Read Hebrews 3:12-14 and 10:24-25. Why do you think discouragement can be a set-up to fall into temptation?

❏ When is the last time you encouraged someone? What steps will you take to encourage others today?

Dave and Joanne Beckwith

Communicate
Truthfully in a Loving Manner

Love is patient, love is kind.
(1 Cor. 13:4)

God can greatly use a word spoken in the right circumstance. Here are principles to communicate in a way that God will use.

1. Speak the truth in love

Truth and love are the perfect balance in communication. *Do not let kindness and truth leave you; bind them around your neck, write them on the tablet of your heart* (Prov. 3:3-5 NASB). If they're around your neck and on your heart, they're with you at all times. Learn balance in your communication. Not every truthful word is kind, and not every kind word is truthful. Paul said, *Speak the truth in love, growing in every way more and more like Christ* (Eph. 4:15 NLT). Growing in Christ-likeness is learning to speak truthfully in love.

How is this applied? When your husband walks in from work and says, "Why's this place always a pigsty when I get home from work?" he sets the tone for a hostile, tense evening. He may have spoken truthfully but certainly not kindly. Instead, if this is an important issue, he should discuss it in a truthful and loving manner, at the right time. "I really value things picked up at home, as it helps me relax and unwind. How could we work together to make this possible?"

While our two daughters were growing up, eating noises were a touchy issue. Without giving away identities, two of us were "munchers," and two were "glarers." Here's how it worked: munchers chewed carrots, granola, apples, celery, or gum with mouth partially open for increased effect, carefully chewing each bite hundreds of times (or so it seemed) to aid digestion. Effectively practiced, it prompted irritated, angry glares. Glarers metaphorically threw deadly daggers across the room without speaking a word. What a crazy issue! After numerous blow-ups, I decided to employ all my skills of international diplomacy. I convinced the glarers to stop stomping out of the room and the munchers to do their crunching in the kitchen. Speaking the truth in love meant saying something like this: "You know, your munching of the carrots is irritating. If you could chew them in the kitchen, I'll look forward to having you rejoin me later."

2. Invite constructive criticism.

Be open to areas where you need to grow. My wife has my invitation to give input that will help me as a person, including critiquing what I wear. One day she said, "You know, that shirt is really out of style." I replied, "Hon, I don't follow the fashions. I set the styles." She shot right back, "Strange that none of those styles have caught on."

Seriously, do yourself a big favor by having someone give you helpful input. *If you profit from constructive criticism, you will be elected to the wise men's hall of fame. But to reject criticism is to harm yourself and your own best interest* (Prov. 15:32 TLB).

3. Share constructive criticism in private.

Is your friend or spouse sensitive or self-conscious about his or her weaknesses? Most of us are. Public embarrassment or ridicule of the other person's fault or idiosyncrasy will inflame bitter resentment. One husband brought up the subject of his wife being overweight at nearly every party they attended. He couldn't understand why she continued to gain weight.

Bob Thune and I met for the first time the night we prayed to receive Christ. He was seven, and I was six years old. Little did we know that years later we'd be in each other's wedding—one day apart. The years in between had much to do with "when weaknesses collide," God's training ground for two future pastors. During high school, we met each morning in the basement of his home to pray before going to band practice. Bob excelled at nearly everything; he was an all-state athlete in football, basketball, and track, and an honor student. I was first-team mediocre in sports and had "by the grace of God" grades. In band, we both played trumpet. I challenged him for first chair and beat him, which meant I sat in front of him. To spite me, he enjoyed filling his trumpet slide with saliva and dumping it on my head.

One morning, I got revenge. While Bob and I were praying in the basement of his home, I arranged for his brother, Rich, to remove his trumpet from the case and fill it with underwear. After taking the trumpet out, Rich packed the case tightly, and when Bob arrived in band he flipped the case open and underwear flew out. He was furious and stomped from the room. To retaliate, he put a firecracker in my back pocket, lit it, and enjoyed my reaction to the explosion. (Don't try this. Serious injury could occur.)

While we were friends, I didn't appreciate Bob's harsh criticism, sometimes done in a room full of other people. But with my uncouth ways, I gave him plenty of ammunition. After his senior year, Bob left for Biola on an athletic scholarship, while I completed my last year of high school in our hometown of Murdo, South Dakota. Toward the end of my senior year, he called me from California and said, "Dave, I want you to come to Biola and be my roommate." My first thought: *What? You want me to room with you? Why? Are you running short on people to criticize?* However, as the phone call continued, I sensed he really wanted to be with me. Rooming together during those college years, our weaknesses—his critical spirit and my defensiveness—began to change, and our relationship grew into a deep friendship. He identified undeveloped potential in my life and often encouraged me.

Four of us roomed together in a quad during college, and these three guys—Bob Thune, Rich Thune, and Howard Parker—had an enormous impact on my life. *As iron sharpens iron, so a friend sharpens a friend* (Prov. 27:17 NLT). We had some hard moments and misunderstandings along the way, but we learned to talk them through. Years later, we're still very close. I see how those three guys practiced the ABC's: 1) They *accepted* me with agape love; 2) They *believed* in my God-surrendered potential; and 3) They *communicated* correction in a truthful, loving manner. Practice the ABC's in a relationship, and you will have a great impact on other lives.

4. Know when to drop an issue.

Don't nag. A kitchen appliance manufacturer received the warranty card sent in by the purchaser. After the question, "What prompted you to buy this appliance?" were three words: *nag, nag, nag*. Proverbs says it's better to live in a desert or an attic than with a crabby, nagging person in a lovely home (Prov. 21:9, 19). In most cases, after clearly communicating a constructive criticism and explaining why it's important, drop it. As

THE EDGE

noted earlier, human nature is such that the very pressure to change usually produces an equal or greater resistance to that change.

5. Give up the myth of perfect compatibility.

Don't expect perfect compatibility. Don't expect a total personality makeover. It's not going to happen. Some of the quirks are the uniqueness of the person. Dr. Francis Schaeffer had a profound influence on Christianity, but his wife, Edith, saw things that irritated her like his muddy boots, being late for dinner, etc. She had to decide: either create an atmosphere of hostility in the home or choose to make the most of every day. She chose the latter. She often lit a candle for dinner and put a slice of lemon in his water, and performed other kindnesses she knew he'd appreciate.

In describing his more than sixty-year marriage, Billy Graham said, "Ruth and I are happily incompatible."

When weaknesses collide, go back to the **ABC's. A**ccept them with unconditional love. **B**elieve in what God will do. **C**ommunicate the truth in love. These are your "loving-edge" to be used by God in a relationship.

Day Five Time Out

Power Thoughts for Your Time Alone with God

If you profit from constructive criticism, you will be elected to the wise men's hall of fame. But to reject criticism is to harm yourself and your own best interest. (Proverbs 15:32 TLB)

- ❏ Read Proverbs 27:5-17.

- ❏ When was the last time someone criticized you? What was your response? How could your response have been better?

- ❏ Identify a time when criticism was just what you needed in your life. How did it cause you to become a stronger person?

- ❏ Who's the sharpening person in your life?

STRENGTH TEAM

SESSION SIX

WHY CAN'T YOU BE MORE LIKE ME?

Differences can be a major source of frustration in relationships often resulting in tension and edginess when you're together. How do you handle being in the same household with an opposite who grates on your nerves? Do you keep quiet or speak up? Does it work to try to change the person? Is there a way to cooperate with God as he works to change someone? In this session, we dig for answers to these questions and more. So let's get started.

CONNECT

- ❏ As a group, take the "Compatibility Quiz" at the start of this chapter. Have someone read each item one at a time and then pause. Raise your hand if it applies to you and you're courageous enough to say so. Elbowing the person next to you is allowed (just don't break any ribs).

GROW

- ❏ This week we're focused on cooperating with God by accepting and affirming one another, believing in what God will do, and communicating the truth in love. Ask four people to read sections of the story of Jonathan and David in 1 Samuel 18:1-4; 19:1-7; 20:35-42; 23:16-18. As you read, discuss how these two men practiced the ABC's in their relationship with each other. Write your observations in the space below.

Accepting each other with unconditional love

Believing in what God will do

Communicating the truth in love

THE EDGE
APPLY

- One at a time, read through the characteristics of love from 1 Corinthians 13 and discuss applying them in your relationships.

    Love is patient with the faults of others (accepting them and trusting God to bring about change in his time).
    Love is kind (gracious, thoughtful, and sensitive to build up rather than tear down).
    Love is not envious (undercutting, spiteful, jealous).
    Love is not boastful (self-centered, pushy to get its own way).
    Love is not proud (not displaying an independent, stubborn spirit, resisting advice, refusing to acknowledge wrongs and ask forgiveness).
    Love is not rude (not insensitive, irritable, touchy, making a scene).
    Love is not self-seeking (instead, it is flexible, gentle, easy to work with, not demanding its own way).
    Love is not easily angered (popping off, easily provoked, hot-headed).
    Love keeps no record of wrongs (does not hold a grudge or bring up the past, but chooses to forgive).
    Love does not delight in evil (divisive, spreading gossip, taking revenge, practicing deceit), *but rejoices with the truth.*
    Love always protects the reputation of others (seeking to give a good report, remaining loyal, and guarding confidential information).
    Love always trusts (believing what God can do).
    Love always hopes (anticipating what God will do).
    Love always perseveres (enduring despite hardships and misunderstandings).
    Love never fails (never giving up or falling away).

- Read aloud in unison the "Changing My Mind" verse for this week.

Accept One Another

Therefore, accept each other just as Christ has accepted you so that God will be given glory.
(Rom. 15:7 NLT)

Changing My Mind – Week 6

PRAY

❑ If group members are in difficult relationships, spend time supporting them in prayer. Both alone and in the group, pray for each other.

❑ With the conclusion of your six weeks together, how will you continue to keep in touch? Do you plan to do another study together?

❑ Has your group considered doing a service project together to share God's love? Painting, cleaning, pruning, repairing? If this is something the group decided to do, you may want to plan a celebration meal together after the service project is completed.

SHARE

❑ Here are some thought-provoking questions that may ignite a discussion this week.

- *What is love?*
- *Have you ever attempted to change someone? How did it work out?*
- *What does it mean to be accepted by another person?*

❑ Be alert to people you meet who are exhausted, discouraged, or frustrated. Look for an opportunity to share an encouraging word of affirmation or listen to them with compassion.

YOUR EDGE TO THRIVE

*Whoever trusts in his riches will fall, but the righteous
will thrive like a green leaf.*
(Prov. 11:28 NIV)

An "edge" may be the cutting side of a knife or the precipice of a dangerous cliff. An "edge" may also be intense vigor and energy—a "cutting-edge" to achieve. Closely related, an "edge" may also refer to keenness and intensity of desire—a "motivational-edge." Weaknesses empowered by God are your "winning-edge" to overcome seemingly insurmountable obstacles.

Here are some final thoughts to hit the road of life with an "edge" to thrive.

1. **Never forget the "edge of ruin" that God pulled you from or kept you from.** What would your life be like left to your own devices? As David said, *You pulled me from the brink of death, my feet from the cliff-edge of doom. Now I stroll at leisure with God in the sunlit fields of life* (Ps. 56:13 MSG).

2. **Be vigilant not to slip back to the "edge of disaster."** It's easy to get careless and fall back into old patterns. Obadiah warned his contemporaries: *All your old partners will drive you to the edge. Your old friends will lie to your face. Your old drinking buddies will stab you in the back. Your world will collapse. You won't know what hit you* (Obad. 1:7 MSG). Keep the cutting-edge of your expectations

sharp. Jesus said, *Be on your guard. Don't let the sharp edge of your expectation get dulled by parties and drinking and shopping* (Luke 21:34 MSG).

3. **Release resentments and regrets.** David said, *I'm on the edge of losing it— the pain in my gut keeps burning* (Ps. 38:17 MSG). You can either live with your teeth on edge and your stomach in a knot, or you can release resentments and regrets before they get a stranglehold on you. Practice forgiveness.

4. **Refuel daily to renew your edge of vigor and energy.** Life will take it out of you—guaranteed. God promises to energize those who get tired, and he gives fresh strength to those who wait on him (Isa. 40:29-31). Meditate daily on the Word of God, and God will give you success in your endeavors (Ps. 1). *Your commands give me an edge on my enemies; they never become obsolete* (Ps. 119:98 MSG). Refuel daily: *You're my place of quiet retreat; I wait for your Word to renew me* (Ps. 119:114 MSG).

5. **Remember the secret of your strength.** God promises, *My power is strongest when you are weak* (2 Cor. 12:9 CEV). Make it your life motto: *When I am weak, I am strong* (2 Cor. 12:10 NLT).

Appendix A

THREE SIMPLE STEPS TO NEW LIFE

Beginning the Christian life is as simple as the ABC's backwards. Today you can begin the most thrilling adventure of your life as a follower of Jesus Christ. Here's how.

Confess your sins. You may have lived a good, moral life, but the Bible says, *All have sinned and fall short of the glory of God* (Rom. 3:23 NASB), and *the wages of sin is death, but the gift of God is eternal life in Christ Jesus our Lord* (Rom. 6:23). The Bible also says, *God showed his great love for us by sending Christ to die for us while we were still sinners* (Rom. 5:8 NLT). Jesus Christ shed his blood on the cross to pay the penalty for your sins and to provide complete forgiveness. Confess your sins and ask Christ to forgive your sins. As the Bible says, *He is patient with you, not wanting anyone to perish, but everyone to come to repentance* (2 Pet. 3:9).

Believe in Jesus Christ as your Savior and Lord. When a religious man asked Jesus how to get to heaven, Jesus told him, *For God so loved the world, that he gave his one and only Son, that whoever believes in him shall not perish but have eternal life* (John 3:16). Believing in Jesus Christ is a simple choice and a step of faith. *If you confess with your mouth that Jesus is Lord and believe in your heart that God raised him from the dead, you will be saved* (Rom. 10:9 NLT).

Accept Christ into your life. The Bible says, *He came to the world that was his own, but his own people did not accept him. But to all who did accept him and believe in him he gave the right to become children of God* (John 1:11–12 NCV). By accepting or asking Christ into your life, he now lives within you. *This is the secret: Christ lives in you* (Col. 1:27 NLT).

"Dear God,
    I confess my sin. Thank you that you forgive every sin because of Christ's death on the cross.
    I believe in Jesus Christ. He proved himself to be God through his miraculous life, his death on the cross, and resurrection from the dead.
    I accept Jesus Christ into my life. By your Spirit, I invite you to live

within me."

_____   _____
Signed   Date

Confess your sins.
Believe in Jesus Christ as your Savior and Lord.
Accept Christ into your life.

Appendix B

THE GROUP FACTOR
A GUIDE FOR SMALL GROUPS

The shared journey is the best journey. If you went on a cruise to Alaska or snorkeling in the Caribbean, would you rather do it alone or have a friend to share it with? When you see something beautiful or experience something spectacular, you naturally want to tell someone about it. God designed us with a need to connect, to share our joys as well as our sorrows with someone who understands. The impact of your six-week personal growth journey will be doubled when others travel with you. Select one or two other people to share the journey with, or develop a small group with several participants. Don't miss the joy of the shared journey.

Why small groups?

In this world driven to achieve big results and big crowds, small groups may seem ... well, small ... as in insignificant and unimportant. God disagrees. The ancient prophet asked, *Who despises the day of small things?* (Zech. 4:10). Small groups are God's idea for fellowship. You can worship with a large crowd, but you can't fellowship with five thousand people. The big crowd fosters loneliness; the small group builds friendships.

Are small groups biblical?

From the earliest days of the Church, the believers met in small groups, usually in someone's home. After the conversion and baptism of 3,000 (recorded in Acts 2:38-41), they began meeting together for teaching, fellowship, prayer, and breaking of bread from house to house (Acts 2:42, 46). This was authentic Christianity at the cell level. As the Church continued to grow and persecution broke out, Acts 5:42 says, *Day after day, in the temple courts and from house to house, they never stopped teaching and proclaiming the good news that Jesus is the Christ.* Before Paul became a follower of Jesus, he was ravaging the Church, going house to house as they met and dragging Christians off to prison (Acts 8:3). After God got hold of his life and spun him around, Paul went from terrorizing believers house to house to teaching believers house to house

(Acts 20:20). Paul also mentions a church in the house of Aquila and Priscilla (Rom. 16:3, 5; 1 Cor. 16:19), Gaius (Rom. 16:23), Philemon (Philem. 1, 2), and Nympha in Laodicea (Col. 4:15).

The intimacy of the home and the dynamic of the small group provide a natural setting for spiritual growth, but groups can meet wherever it works—a coffee shop, restaurant, at the work place, or in a park. You name the setting, and Jesus will meet you there. A small group can be two or three people or as many as twelve to fifteen. And remember, the Lord is present whenever you meet. The presence of Jesus makes your group, large or small, an exciting place to be.

TIPS FOR LEADING A SMALL GROUP

Being a facilitator for a small group is not as difficult as it may seem. You don't have to be a preacher or even a great talker. If you're taking the lead in a small group, here are some tips.

1. **Prepare in advance.** Read the Bible passages, think through the questions, and pray for the members of the group before each session.

2. **Don't do it all yourself.** Before you begin, if possible, select a co-leader to assist you and to lead from time to time. Have someone else coordinate a refreshment schedule so everyone brings something. You may also want to rotate homes.

3. **Introduce newcomers.** Make certain everyone knows the others in the group by name. The "Connect" section that opens each session is designed to facilitate knowing each other personally and deepening your relationships.

4. **Prepare a group roster.** Have a group member make a list of the names, phone numbers, and email addresses of group members and distribute a copy to each person. Don't forget to update it when a new person joins the group. We've provided a worksheet titled "God's VIPs" for your group roster.

5. **Relax and be who you are.** Rather than worrying about the impression you're making on others, greet each person with a warm smile. Be interested in them and enjoy laughing together. If someone asks a question you don't have an answer to, say so. You don't have to be a know-it-all. They will respect you for being a learner with them.

6. **Ask questions and listen.** Being an effective group leader is more about listening than telling. The questions included with each session are designed for discussion. If you add questions of your own, don't use closed-ended questions. These are questions that are answered with a "yes" or "no" or require no more than a one-or-two-word answer. They close off discussion. Instead, use open-ended questions. For example, "Why do you think this is important?" or "How did you feel when …?" or "What would you recommend to someone facing this situation?" Don't panic if you ask a question and there isn't an immediate response. Be patient as group members gather their thoughts.

7. **Rotate around the group for Scripture reading.** To involve everyone, have each person read one or two verses.

8. **Affirm the responses of group members.** After someone shares, show your appreciation by saying something like, "Thanks for sharing that" or "That was a helpful insight." Then for those who haven't shared, ask "Would someone else like to add to this?" or "We haven't had the opportunity to hear from everyone on this. Who else would like to share?" Even if someone gives a wrong answer, don't put them down. Gently give another perspective. Be sensitive to those who are new or reluctant to speak up or pray out loud. Give them a safe place; as they feel comfortable, they'll come along. Don't force or pressure them.

9. **Don't allow one or two people to dominate the discussion.** If an individual is taking over the discussion, say something like, "Thank you, Joe, for sharing. And since we haven't heard from the others, let's hear what they have to offer." If it continues to be a problem, meet alone with him, where you can say something like, "Joe, I'm pleased you're part of the group, and you have good things to share. However, I want to ask you to help me help the quieter members participate equally. Please give a brief comment, and then let's pass the opportunity to others."

10. **Break into smaller groups.** If your group is larger than seven people, divide into smaller groups of two to four people for part of the session. This is also an effective setting for prayer. The quieter person will feel more comfortable praying out loud when the group is smaller. This smaller group can become a "prayer partnership." Encourage them to be in touch during the week by phone, email, or text.

11. **Pray and worship together.** Allow individuals to share their prayer concerns and then take the time to pray for each other. Encourage short prayers. Occasionally you may want the group to pray using one-sentence prayers. This can be particularly effective when praising God for his attributes and blessings. Sometimes you'll want to stand and join hands in a circle as you pray. This creates a strong sense of unity. Music can also be a vital part of prayer. If someone

plays an instrument, you can ask them to lead in a simple song of praise. Or you can select a song on a Christian CD and play it as the group sings along. Make certain the song is not too difficult for singing as a group.

12. **Go with the flow.** It isn't necessary to cover all the questions. Be flexible, but make certain the meeting doesn't go too long. A good discussion can continue after the group is dismissed if this is acceptable to the host.[51]

Tips for Hosting a Small Group

The thought of others coming to your home can be quite intimidating. If you're uptight about making a good impression, you will have difficulty enjoying the group. Instead of feeling you have to entertain your guests, choose to relax and give hospitality to your guests. Here are the crucial differences.

Entertaining versus showing hospitality

There is a world of difference between entertaining and hospitality. Entertaining seeks to impress others; hospitality seeks to be interested in others. When you're entertaining, you're constantly asking yourself, "What are they thinking? Am I making a good impression?" With hospitality, the focus is on your guest, not on yourself. Ask caring questions. Listen with love and understanding. Often, entertaining creates a pressure to perform, which then creates fear and nervousness. Hospitality is different. You can tell when you're practicing hospitality because it will almost always be a joyful experience. You sense God using you to show love to others. Peter reminded the believers, *Most importantly, love each other deeply, because love will cause many sins to be forgiven. Open your homes to each other, without complaining* (1 Pet. 4:8-9 NCV).

What is important for your guests?

Think through the last time you were invited as a guest to someone's home. Check below what was *essential* for you to feel comfortable and welcomed. This will help you know what is really important when people come to your home.

Yes	No	Maybe	
____	____	____	Home spotlessly clean and closets organized
____	____	____	Silver tea service, imported cups and saucers
____	____	____	Feeling the host was glad you came
____	____	____	Windows washed and carpets cleaned
____	____	____	Furnishings that could be featured in *Home & Decor*
____	____	____	Host asks how your week has been
____	____	____	Home comfortably clean
____	____	____	Fresh-cut flowers
____	____	____	Gourmet entrees and expensive desserts
____	____	____	Relaxed setting
____	____	____	Feeling accepted as a person
____	____	____	Healthy and tasty snacks
____	____	____	Kick-your-shoes-off comfortable
____	____	____	Being listened to

Five Purposes for Your Group

Each group session has five sections, and each section is designed with a specific purpose in mind. Using the five purposes taught by Pastor Rick Warren in his book *The Purpose Driven Life*, each session includes these five purposes: fellowship, discipleship, ministry, evangelism, and worship. These five purposes give a clear direction to each session, and they also provide balance. For example, a group may drift into just being a social gathering or fall into "in-grown-itis"—caring only for themselves. These dangers and others can be prevented by including all five purposes in each session. (You will notice these five sections in each session.)

1. **Connect** (fellowship): This section is designed for you to get to know each other and deepen your friendships. As the Bible says, *Love each other, be deep-spirited friends* (Phil. 2:2 MSG). Love is the flag flying high that identifies you as a true follower of Christ: *Your love for one another will prove to the world that you are my disciples* (John 13:35 NLT).

THE EDGE

2. **Grow** (discipleship): This section is designed for you to dig into God's Word. Questions are designed to help you think through the biblical meaning of a passage. Jesus said, *If you continue in my word, then you are truly disciples of mine; and you will know the truth, and the truth will make you free* (John 8:31-32 NASB).

3. **Apply** (ministry): Questions in this section are designed to apply God's Word to your life and give you specific ways to serve others in love. Peter reminded the believers: *God has given each of you a gift from his great variety of spiritual gifts. Use them well to serve one another* (1 Pet. 4:10 NLT).

4. **Pray** (worship): Jesus said, *If two of you on earth agree about anything you ask for, it will be done for you by my Father in heaven* (Matt. 18:19). Use this time to praise God, share answers to prayer, and pray for the needs in the group.

5. **Share** (evangelism): This section is designed to help you share your faith with your contacts during the week. As the Scripture says, *Always be prepared to give an answer to everyone who asks you to give the reason for the hope that you have. But do this with gentleness and respect* (1 Pet. 3:15). Questions are included in this section for you to start a conversation to share your faith during the week.

Dave and Joanne Beckwith

SMALL GROUP GUIDELINES

To keep things on track, it is helpful for the group to commit to some practices that make for a healthy group. At the beginning of a new study, read through these guidelines, discuss, and agree to practice them. This may be duplicated for the group.

- ❑ **Stay Focused and Balanced:** We meet to worship God, fellowship together, grow in the Word of God, apply the Word to our life to serve others, and share our faith with unbelievers.

- ❑ **Group Attendance:** To stay in touch with one another, we will call, text, or send an email if we are unable to attend or running late. This will be our goal for when the group starts and ends: Arrival time: _____ Starting time: _____ Ending time: _____

    These are the calendar dates we will be meeting: _____

- ❑ **Guard Confidences:** We will be careful to avoid sharing confidential information outside the group.

- ❑ **Healthy Group Life:** We will be careful to avoid dominating the conversation, and we will always look for the opportunity for everyone to share. We will seek to make this a safe place where others can share their struggles without receiving a snap judgment or a quick fix to their problem. We will be sensitive to the special needs of group members—some may have to leave for work at 4:30 a.m., so we will be careful not to go too late; some may have dietary restrictions so we will be alert to these when planning refreshments or a meal together; and some may be struggling with alcohol so we recognize it is best to not serve alcoholic beverages.

- ❑ **Welcome Newcomers:** We will look for opportunities to invite friends and warmly welcome newcomers to the group.

THE EDGE
ASK AND YOU SHALL RECEIVE

Jesus said, *You may ask me for anything in my name, and I will do it* (John 14:14). This was so important, so strategic, that Jesus repeated it six times in his final night with his disciples before his crucifixion (John 14:13, 14, 15:7, 16; 16:24, 26). The promise is yours today: *ask and you shall receive.* As a group, share your prayer requests and praise reports. This is a place to write down those requests and to make notes of answers to prayer. This may be duplicated for the group.

Date	Pray Request	Answer to Prayer

GOD'S VIPS
MEMBERS OF YOUR SMALL GROUP
(This may be duplicated for use in a small group)

Name and Contact Information **Phone Contact**

Name: _____ (___) _____ Cell

Email: _____ (___) _____ Home

Name: _____ (___) _____ Cell

Email: _____ (___) _____ Home

Name: _____ (___) _____ Cell

Email: _____ (___) _____ Home

Name: _____ (___) _____ Cell

Email: _____ (___) _____ Home

Name: _____ (___) _____ Cell

Email: _____ (___) _____ Home

Name: _____ (___) _____ Cell

Email: _____ (___) _____ Home

Name: _____ (___) _____ Cell

Email: _____ (___) _____ Home

Name: _____ (___) _____ Cell

Email: _____ (___) _____ Home

Name: _____ (___) _____ Cell

Email: _____ (___) _____ Home

Name: _____ (___) _____ Cell

Email: _____ (___) _____ Home

Appendix C

DIGGING DEEPER

HOW GOD'S WORD WILL CHANGE MY LIFE

If you have additional time, enjoy reading Psalm 119, the longest chapter in the Bible and the classic section on how God's Word will change your life. Make a list of your observations in two categories. Add additional pages if needed. Some examples are included to get you started.

Benefits of God's Word	**My Responses to God's Word**
God's Word will …	**I will …**
bless me: vv. 1, 2	seek him: vv. 2, 10
keep me from being put to shame: v. 6	obey: vv. 4, 8, 17
keep me from sin: vv. 9, 11	hide the word in my heart: v. 11

Appendix D

RELEASING RESENTMENTS

This is a walk-through of the steps to release resentments. Use this worksheet or a separate sheet of paper, which may be destroyed later. Don't overlook resentments that may be decades old. You may copy this worksheet for yourself or your small group.

Description of a Resentment (Injustice, Mistreatment, Pain, Circumstance)	**Type of Resentment** (1, 2, 3, 4)	**Are you willing to forgive?**	**Placed on "God's-to-Do" list**

Appendix E

RELEASING REGRETS

This is a walk-through of the steps to release regrets. Use this worksheet or a separate sheet of paper, which may be destroyed later. Think through regrets that linger in your mind. Be specific. You may copy this worksheet for yourself or your small group.

My Regrets Actions, attitudes, words spoken	Apology completed if needed	I agree with God's forgiveness	I am forgiven & set free

MEDITATION AND MEMORY VERSES

God's Power Pack
I can do all things through him who strengthens me. Greater is he who is in me than he who is in the world. I am more than a conqueror through him who loves me. Absolutely nothing is impossible with God!
(First person paraphrase from Phil. 4:13; 1 John 4:4; Rom. 8:37; Luke 1:37)

Changing My Mind – Week 1

Power Perfected in Weakness
"My grace is sufficient for you, for my power is made perfect in weakness." Therefore I will boast all the more gladly about my weaknesses, so that Christ's power may rest on me. (2 Cor. 12:9 NIV)

Changing My Mind – Week 2

A Mental Makeover
Don't copy the behavior and customs of this world, but let God transform you into a new person by changing the way you think. (Rom. 12:2 NLT)

Changing My Mind – Week 3

Weed Killer for a Bitter Root

Look after each other so that none of you fails to receive the grace of God. Watch out that no poisonous root of bitterness grows up to trouble you, corrupting many.
(Heb. 12:15 NLT)

Changing My Mind – Week 4

Blameless

For he chose us in him before the creation of the world to be holy and blameless in his sight.
(Eph. 1:4 NIV)

Changing My Mind – Week 5

Accept One Another

Therefore, accept each other just as Christ has accepted you so that God will be given glory.
(Rom. 15:7 NLT)

Changing My Mind – Week 6

ABOUT THE AUTHORS
DAVE AND JOANNE BECKWITH

One week after their wedding in 1969, Dave and Joanne began their journey in pastoral ministry. And what an adventure it has been—some thrilling joys and successes along with struggles and setbacks. While on a youth trip in their second year of ministry, they were rescued from a fiery head-on freeway collision with a drunk driver—driving on the wrong side of the freeway. Years later, Dave miraculously survived a 40-foot fall, an experience God used to correct and redirect him.

Dave's ministry experience includes camp and youth ministry, church administration, and serving as a senior pastor for over thirty years. Joanne has been an active partner in the ministry, working alongside Dave while leading women's ministries, mentoring, and teaching small groups. Currently, Dave is pastor emeritus for Woodbridge Church in Irvine, California, where he served as senior pastor for nearly twenty years. He also serves as a lead pastor for churches going through transition and a small-group leader and story writer for Saddleback Church.

Dave and Joanne are both graduates of Biola University. Joanne received her bachelor's degree in nursing. Professionally, she has worked in alcohol and drug rehab and psychiatry with short and long term patients. The last 14 years have been with Kaiser Permanente. Dave received his bachelor's degree in business administration at Biola and completed his seminary work at Talbot Theological Seminary. Additional graduate studies have included an MA in Biblical Studies and PhD in Church and Family Ministry.

Their two married daughters, Julie and Tami, and four grandchildren and four great-grandchildren are a source of joy and entertainment in their lives. A love for God's beauty in nature takes them on hikes and rides on their recumbent bikes. They especially love sunsets at the ocean.

Having faced the painful side of personal and church life has equipped them to come alongside others. God has given them a heart for those who hurt, and a shared life mission to help others discover God's power in their weakest moments. One of their greatest joys is sharing a cup of coffee or a meal—weeping with those who weep, and rejoicing with those who rejoice.

You may contact them at:
Standing Stone Ministry
P.O. Box 434
Balboa Island, CA 92662
www.standingstoneministry.org or www.pastorbiker.com
dave.b@standingstoneministry.org
joanne.b@standingstoneministry.org

ENDNOTES

The Edge

1. *Merriam-Webster's Dictionary and Thesaurus, Macmillan Dictionary*

Chapter One: When Life Hits You Head-on

2. Dennis Sprik speaks in churches, schools, and camps presenting the "Hands of the Potter" program. While speaking, Dennis shapes jars of clay to illustrate Jeremiah 18:6. Dave and Dennis have teamed together combining Dave's story with the "Hands of the Potter" program (www.handsofthepotter.net).

Chapter Two: Why Did God Design Me with Weaknesses?

3. Miles J. Stanford, *The Complete Green Letters* (Grand Rapids, Mich: Zondervan Publishing, 1975), p. 5.

4. Miles J. Stanford, p. 16.

5. Miles J. Stanford, p. 16.

6. Phil. 4:13, 1 John 4:4, Rom. 8:37, and Luke 1:37 first person paraphrase.

7. Jon Kabat-Zinn wrote a book titled *Wherever You Go, There You Are* (New York: Hyperion, 1994).

8. www.gallupstrengthscenter.com

9. I first heard this general thought in a message by Pastor Adrian Rogers, Pastor of a Southern Baptist Church and President of the SBC Convention, at Bethel College's Founders Week, Jan. 23-26, 1984.

10. Paul David Tripp, *Dangerous Calling* (Wheaton, IL: Crossway, 2012), p. 33.

11. Miles J. Stanford, *The Complete Green Letters* (Grand Rapids, MI: Zondervan 1975), p. 6.

12. James Goggin and Kyle Strobel, *Beloved Dust* (Nashville, Tenn: Nelson Books, 2014), p. 43.

13. Jack Miller, www.goodreads.com/author/quotes

14. *Mosby's Medical Dictionary,* 8th edition. © 2009, Elsevier.

15. *The MacArthur Study Bible*

16. *Life Application Bible, 1 and 2 Corinthians.*

Chapter Three: Changing My Mind

17. One of the earlier references to this quote is in a book review article by Robert Sherrill in the *New York Times,* "Titles in the Running for 1972," February 13, 1972.

18. Daniel G. Amen, M.D., *Change Your Brain, Change Your Body* (New York: Harmony Books, 2010), p. 17.

19. Carl Zimmer, "Secrets of the Brain," *National Geographic,* Vol. 225, No. 2, Feb. 2014, p. 37.

20. J. D. Ratcliff, "I Am Joe's Brain," *Reader's Digest* (April 1974), p. 91.

21. Ratcliff, p. 93.

22. *Human Brain: Amazing Facts,* May 13, 2010.

23. "Willard's Brain," *Campus Life* (September 1988), p. 40.

24. "Willard's Brain," p. 40.

25. Daniel G. Amen, M.D., *Change Your Brain, Change Your Body* (New York: Harmony Books, 2010), p. 237.

26. John W. Drakeford, *Counseling for Church Leaders* (Nashville: Broadman Press, 1961), p. 16.

27. Daniel G. Amen, M.D., *Change Your Brain, Change Your Body* (New York: Harmony Books, 2010), p. 237.

28. "Willard's Brain," p. 40.

29. Daniel Amen, M.D., *Change Your Brain, Change Your Life* (New York: Three Rivers Press, 1998), pp. 8-9. For further study, Dr. Amen identifies different parts of the brain and how they affect behavior. The deep limbic system is the bonding and mood control center, the basal ganglia controls anxiety, panic, fearfulness, and conflict avoidance, the prefrontal cortex is the part of the brain that makes plans, controls impulses, and makes decisions, the singulate is the "gear shifter" that allows for moving from one thought to another, and the temporal lobes are involved with memory, facial recognition, and understanding language. Dr. Amen prescribes treatments for each region of the brain and how to deal with various issues such as anxiety, depression, ADD, obsessive behavior, and anger.

30. "Butterfly," *World Book Encyclopedia*, 2007.

31. J. I. Packer, *Knowing God* (Downers Grove, IL: InterVarsity Press, 1973), pp. 18-19.

32. William M. Struthers, *Wired for Intimacy: How Pornography Hijacks the Male Brain* (Downers Grove, IL: InterVarsity Press, 2009), pp. 85, 106.

33. "Porn: the New Drug," *afaJournal*, Oct. 2014, Vol. 38, No. 9, p. 4

34. "Code of Practices for Television Broadcasters Television History - The First 75 Years," *Wikipedia Encyclopedia*

35. Vitagliano, "TV's fall," *afaJournal,* Vol. 38, No. 8, Sept. 2014.

36. Vangie Beal, "How to Completely Erase a Hard Disk Drive," www.webopedia.com.

Chapter Four: Releasing Resentments

37. Rabbi Yehuda Berg, "Motivational Quotes," http://www.motivationalquotesabout.com/from/yehuda-berg

38. S. I. McMillen, M.D., *None of These Diseases* (Old Tappen, New Jersey: Fleming H. Revell Co., 1967), p. 72.

39. John Parker, *Tour of Bible Lands,* 1975.

Chapter Five: Releasing Resentments

40. Stephen Pile, *The Incomplete Book of Failures* (New York; E. P. Dutton, 1979), pp. 39-40.

41. C. S. Lewis, *God in the Dock*, "Cross-Examination" (1963), paragraph 44, p. 265. C. S. Lewis is often quoted as saying in *Screwtape Letters*, "It is Satan's strategy to get a Christian preoccupied with their failures; from then on the battle is won." It is a great truth, though it is not found in the *Screwtape Letters.*

42. Max Lucado, *God Came Near* (Portland: Multnomah Press, 1987), p. 73.

43. Haddon W. Robinson, "The Gospel of the Second Chance," *Moody Monthly* (February 1979), pp. 71-72.

Chapter Six: Why Can't You Be More Like Me?

44. Adapted from Dave Beckwith, "The Ultimate Compatibility Quiz," *Marriage Partnership,* Fall 1991, p. 37.

THE EDGE

45. This was quoted by Earl Nightingale, "How to React to Stress," Nightingale-Conant, 1400 South Wolf Road, Bldg. 300, Suite 103, Wheeling, IL 60090, http://www.nightingale.com. The research was originally done by Dr. Hans Selye, Canadian physician and scientist who pioneered stress research.

46. Kenneth S. Wuest, *Bypaths in the Greek New Testament* (Grand Rapids, Mich: Wm. B. Eerdmans Publishing Co., 1940), pp. 109-110.

47. Bruce W. Thielemann, "Gayle Sayers and Brian Piccolo: Crossing Racial Lines," *Preaching Today,* Tuesday, May 16, 2000, Tape No. 40.

48. Kenneth S. Wuest, *Golden Nuggets from the Greek New Testament* (Grand Rapids, Mich: Wm. B. Eerdmans Publishing Co., 1940), p. 60.

49. Janie B. Cheaney, "Male call," *WORLD,* September 5, 2011, p. 20.

50. Thayer, *Greek-English Lexicon of the New Testament,* p. 25.

The Group Factor: A Guide for Small Groups

51. General thoughts are adapted from Rick Warren, *Developing a Faith That Works, Volume 1* (Saddleback Resources, 30021 Comercio, Rancho Santa Margarita, CA 92688, www.saddlebackresources.com), pp. 60-63.

SCRIPTURE INDEX

Genesis
2:23—225
37:19-36—149 *
50:18-20—149 *
50:20—149

Exodus
24:18—13

Numbers
11:1—141
11:1-6—139
11:11-15—146
11:13-15—140, 146

Deuteronomy
6:6-9—113, 115 *

Joshua
1:6-9—110, 111, 134

1 Samuel
2:7—146
18:1, 3-4—225
18:1-4—242
19:1-7—242
20:35-42—242
23:16-18—242
25:37-38—150

2 Samuel
11:1-17—198 **
11:1-27—177 *

1 Kings
18:38—140
19:8—13

Psalms
1:1-3—115 *
1:2-3—111, 135
2:12—194
17:8—125
18:2—33, 35
18:1-6—35 *
19:14—122, 136
23:1-6—23 *
23:1-6—43 **
32:1—198
32:1-2—196, 201
32:8-9—190
38:4-10—173-174
38:17—150, 246
38:18—182
50:19-20—178
51:1-19—195 *
55:12-14—144
55:20-21—144
56:13—245
59:7—150
71:1—193
81:12—223
103:11-12—187
119:1-176—259
119:11—111, 112, 134
119:98—126
119:114—124, 246
119:70—112
119:92—113
119:98—133, 246
138:8—63
139:1-6—99-100
139:1-6, 23-24—103 *
139:2—92
139:13-14—63
139:13-18—95 *
139:14—91

Proverbs
3:3-5—234
4:23—116, 132
4:23, 25—116
8:10—97
11:28—245
11:29—150
12:8—96
15:1—55
15:32—235, 239
16:18—72
17:17—219, 228
21:9, 19—236
27:5—229
27:5-17—239 *
27:6—219, 228
27:17—236
28:13—182
28:14—213
28:26—228

Song of Solomon
8:6-7—223

Ecclesiastes
3:11—216

Isaiah
1:18—182
26:3—111, 135
38:17—187
40:29—11, 36
40:29-31—246
40:31—37
43:25—63, 187, 196, 201
44:8—33, 35
45:9—146
53:5—28
54:10—63

Jeremiah
13:17—223
29:11—33, 35
29:11-13—190
31:34—186
32:27—33, 35

Obadiah
1:7—245

Jonah
3:4—13

Micah
7:19—187

Zechariah
4:10—249

Matthew
4:2—13
5:3-10—57 *
5:23-24—183
5:23-24—185 *
6:14-15—158
6:9-15—136 *
7:1-5—178
9:4—92
18:19—255

Mark
9:2-3—105

Luke
1:37—46, 265 ***
19:8—184
21:34—245-246

John
1:11-12—247
3:16—247
8:31-32—255
13:35—254
14:13-14—257
15:7, 16—257
15:12-13—221
16:24, 26—257

Acts
1:3—13
2:38-41—249
2:42, 46—249
3:19—187
5:42—249
8:3—249
13:22—193
16:24—185
20:20—250

Romans
1:24-32—116
1:28—96
1:28-31—116-117
1:31—218
2:1—179
3:23—247
5:8—247
6:23—247
7:15—62, 145
7:15-19—86 **
7:18—62
8:1—190
8:28-39—39
8:31-39—39
8:37—46, 265 ***
10:9—247
10:17—111, 134
12:1-2—104, 111, 134
12:1-2—109 *
12:2—105, 106, 120, 122, 124
12:2—134, 265 ***
12:3—73
12:6-8—66
12:6-16—209 *
12:10—219
15;1-7, 13—227 *
15:7—63
15:7—244, 266 ***
16:3, 5—250
16:23—250

1 Corinthians
1:25-28—13
1:25-31—71 *
1:26-27—67-68
2:9-10—123
2:14—123
2:16—106, 123
11:23-26—202
12:1—66
12:8-10, 28—66
13:4—234
13:4-13—223, 224
13:5—167

13:7—217, 228
15:43-44—75
16:19—250

2 Corinthians
1:8-9—53
3:4-6—53
3:18—105
4:1, 16—53
4:7—53
4:8-9—53
4:10—79
4:16—53
4:17—53
6:10—53
7:4—232
7:10—182
8:24—232
10:3-5—122
10:4-5—101
10:5—102
10:17-18—80
11:16-30—80
11:24-29—58
11:29—81
12:1-6—80
12:1-7—72, 73
12:7—72, 86-87
12:7-8—51
12:7-10—72
12:7-10—86 **
12:7-10—77 *
12:9—36, 51, 58,
   73, 79, 81, 86
12:9—87, 265 ***
12:9—246
12:9-10—74, 81
12:9-19—18
12:10—58, 78, 246
12:11-12—80

Galatians
1:16-18—69
6:4—232
6:11—51
6:14—79

Ephesians
1:3-14—65 *
1:4—63, 186
1:4—200, 266 ***
1:4-5—124
2:4—63
2:4-5—221
4:11-12—66
4:15—234
4:25-32—159 *
4:29—125

Philippians
2:2—254
2:14-15—141
3:3—67
3:4—67
3:4-10—86 **
3:7—68
3:7-8—68
3:10—36
4:4-8—129 *
4:4-9—133 **
4:6-8—111, 135
4:7—111, 135
4:8—121
4:11-12—73
4:13—37
4:13—46, 265 ***
5:25—223

Colossians
1:22—186
1:27—247
3:1-10—83 *
3:3, 5—78
4:15—250

1 Thessalonians
5:18—80

1 Timothy
1:20—157
1:12-20—181 *
1:19—185
4:14-18—86 **

6:6, 17—73
6:10—67

2 Timothy
3:3—218
4:9-18—58
4:9-18—166-167 **
4:14—157, 159
4:16—156

Philemon
1, 2—250

Hebrews
3:12-14—233 *
3:13—229
4:12-13—98, 122
4:16—186-187
10:24-25—233*
11:6—186
12:1-2—190
12:1-3, 14-15—153*
12:15—50
12:15—168, 266 ***

James
1:2—27
1:2-5—27
1:2-12—27 *
3:13-18—215 *
3:14—154
4:7—191
4:10—69
5:7-18—143 *
5:13-20—189 *
5:16—189
5:19—141

1 Peter
1:3-9—31 *
1:6-7—29
2:24—157
3:15—136, 255
4:8-9—253
4:9-11—66
4:10—66, 255

5:7—63

2 Peter 3:9—247

1 John
1:9—63, 182, 189
2:1—187
4:4—46, 265 ***
4:16—221

Revelation
12:10—191

* Time Out Daily
  Reading
** Strength Team
  Study
*** Meditation Verse

Made in the USA
San Bernardino, CA
19 February 2019